HMH

math
expressions
Common Core

Dr. Karen C. Fuson

Watch the platypus come alive in its watery world as you discover and solve math challenges.

Download the Math Expressions AR app available on Android or iOS devices.

Grade 2
Volume 2

This material is based upon work supported by the
National Science Foundation
under Grant Numbers
ESI-9816320, REC-9806020, and RED-935373.

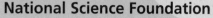

Any opinions, findings, and conclusions, or recommendations expressed in this material
are those of the author and do not necessarily reflect the views of the National Science Foundation.

BIG IDEA 3 - Word Problems: Addition and Subtraction Within 100

BIG IDEA 1 - Arrays and Equal Shares

BIG IDEA 2 - Relate Addition and Subtraction to Length

Student Resources

difference

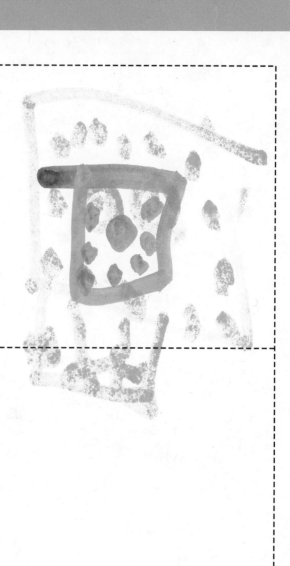

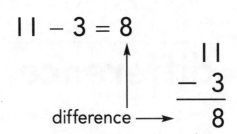

$$11 - 3 = 8$$

difference $\longrightarrow$
$$\begin{array}{r} 11 \\ -\ 3 \\ \hline 8 \end{array}$$

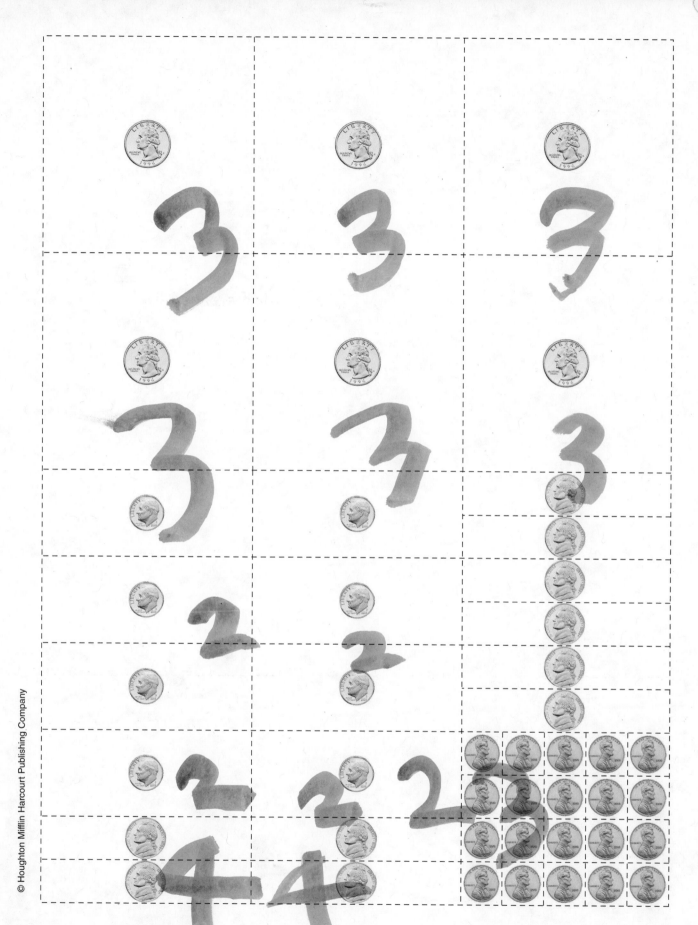

Cut on dashed lines.

Coin Cards

Name _Hanza 3/12/18_

Make 25 Cents

Draw the correct coins to show 25¢.

1 pennies

25

2 nickels

25

3 dimes and nickels

4 any coins

Find the Money Amount

Read the sentence. Draw the coins.
Find the total amount.

5 Louise has 2 quarters
and 1 dime.

_____ ¢

6 Ned has 5 dimes and
3 nickels.

65 ¢

7 Vic has 4 nickels and
5 pennies.

25 ¢

8 Olga has 3 quarters
and 9 pennies.

84 ¢

 Check Understanding

Explain how to show 53 cents using only
quarters and pennies.

Explore Quarters

Cut on dashed lines.

Dollar Equivalents (front) **197**

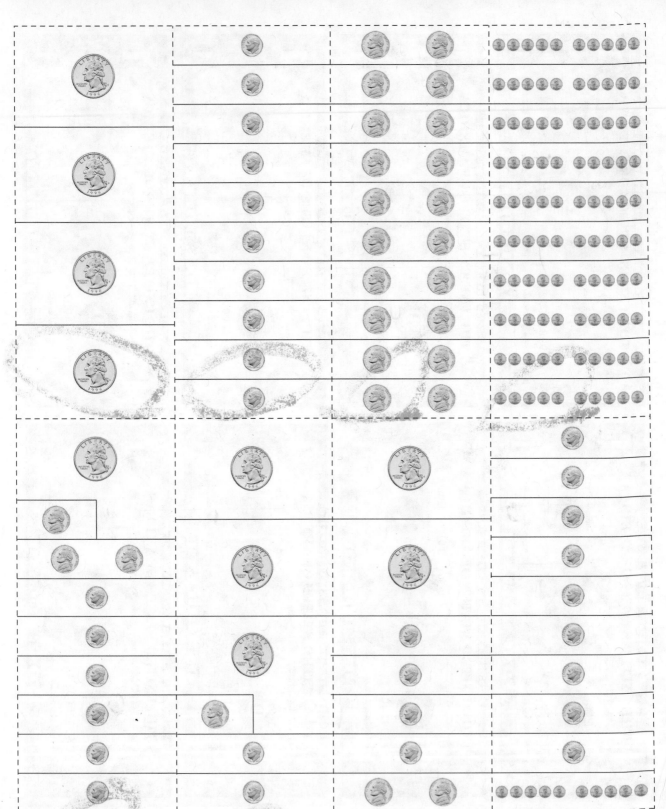

Cut only on dashed lines.

Dollar Equivalents (bⵁ)

Name _____

Count Coins and Bills

Under each picture, write the total amount of money so far.
Then write the total using $. The first exercise is done for you.

1

25¢   25¢   10¢   5¢

25¢   50¢   60¢   65¢

$ _0_ . _6_ _5_
total

2

25¢   10¢   10¢   1¢   1¢

25   3̶5   45   46   47

$ 0.47
total

3

100¢   25¢   5¢   5¢

1.00   1̶25   1.30   1.35

$ 0.35
total

4 Bo has 1 dollar, 2 quarters, 1 dime, 4 nickels, and 3 pennies.
Draw [100] s, (25) s, (10) s, (5) s, and (1) s.

    OO   9   OOOO   OOO

Write the total amount of money.

$ 0.83
total

CC SS Content Standards **2.NBT.B.7, 2.MD.C.8**
Mathematical Practices **MP1, MP3, MP6**

What's the Error?

100¢   1¢   1¢

$ __1__ . __2__

I wrote the total. Did I make a mistake?

5 Show Puzzled Penguin how you would find the total amount of money. Under each picture, write the total amount so far.

100¢   1¢   1¢

_____   _____   _____ $ _____ . _____
                                                     total

More Practice Writing Totals

6 100¢   5¢   1¢   1¢

_____   _____   _____   _____ $ _____ . _____
                                                       total

✓ **Check Understanding**

What is the value of 1 dollar bill, 2 quarters, 3 dimes, 2 nickels, and 1 penny?

_____

Explore Dollars

Name _____ Date _____

Under the picture, write the total amount so far. Use ¢.
Then write the total using $.

①   25¢   25¢   10¢   10¢   10¢   10¢   5¢   1¢

   25¢   50¢   60¢   70¢   80¢   90¢   95¢   96

$ 0 . 9 6

total

②   100¢   25¢   10¢   5¢   5¢

       100¢   125¢   135¢   140   145

$ 0 . 1 45

total

③ Abbie has 1 dollar, 1 quarter, 1 dime, 2 nickels, and
3 pennies. Draw ⬜100 s, ㉕s, ⑩s, ⑤s, ①s.
Write the total amount of money.

$ 1 . 4 8

total

Name _____ Date _____

Add or subtract.

1. $4 + 3 = \boxed{7}$ 2. $11 + 7 = \boxed{18}$ 3. $9 + 5 = \boxed{14}$

4. $12 - 6 = \boxed{6}$ 5. $10 - 6 = \boxed{4}$ 6. $17 - 9 = \boxed{8}$

7.
$$\begin{array}{r} 14 \\ -12 \\ \hline 2 \end{array}$$

8.
$$\begin{array}{r} 14 \\ -\ 6 \\ \hline 8 \end{array}$$

9.
$$\begin{array}{r} 20 \\ -\ 9 \\ \hline 11 \end{array}$$

10.
$$\begin{array}{r} 40 \\ +10 \\ \hline 50 \end{array}$$

11.
$$\begin{array}{r} 30 \\ +38 \\ \hline 68 \end{array}$$

12.
$$\begin{array}{r} 53 \\ +17 \\ \hline 70 \end{array}$$

13.
$$\begin{array}{r} 54 \\ +38 \\ \hline 92 \end{array}$$

14.
$$\begin{array}{r} 71 \\ +13 \\ \hline 84 \end{array}$$

15.
$$\begin{array}{r} 62 \\ +38 \\ \hline 100 \end{array}$$

Dear Family:

In this program, children learn these two methods for 2-digit subtraction. However, children may use any method that they understand, can explain, and can do fairly quickly.

Expanded Method	Ungroup First Method
Step 1 "Expand" each number to show that it is made up of tens and ones. $$64 = 60 + 4$$ $$-28 = 20 + 8$$ **Step 2** Check to see if there are enough ones to subtract from. If not, ungroup a ten into 10 ones and add it to the existing ones. $$64 = \overset{50}{\cancel{60}} + \overset{14}{\cancel{4}}$$ $$-28 = 20 + 8$$ **Step 3** Subtract to find the answer. Children may subtract from left to right or from right to left. $$64 = \overset{50}{\cancel{60}} + \overset{14}{\cancel{4}}$$ $$-28 = 20 + 8$$ $$\overline{30 + 6 = 36}$$	**Step 1** Check to see if there are enough ones to subtract from. If not, ungroup by opening up one of the 6 tens in 64 to be 10 ones. 4 ones plus these new 10 ones make 14 ones. We draw a magnifying glass around the top number to help children focus on the regrouping.  **Step 2** Subtract to find the answer. Children may subtract from left to right or from right to left. 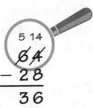

In explaining any method they use, children are expected to use "tens and ones" language. This shows that they understand they are subtracting 2 tens from 5 tens (not 2 from 5) and 8 ones from 14 ones.

Please contact me if you have any questions or comments.

Sincerely,
Your child's teacher

CC SS Unit 4 addresses the following standards from the Common Core State Standards for Mathematics: **2.OA.A.1, 2.OA.B.2, 2.NBT.A.4, 2.NBT.B.5, 2.NBT.B.6, 2.NBT.B.7, 2.NBT.B.8, 2.NBT.B.9, 2.MD.C.8, and all** Mathematical Practices.

Estimada familia:

En este programa, los niños aprenden estos dos métodos para restar con números de 2 dígitos. Sin embargo, pueden usar cualquier método que comprendan, puedan explicar y puedan hacer relativamente rápido.

Método extendido	Método de desagrupar primero
Paso 1 "Extender" cada número para mostrar que consta de decenas y unidades. $$64 = 60 + 4$$ $$-28 = 20 + 8$$ **Paso 2** Observar si hay suficientes unidades para restar. Si no las hay, desagrupar una decena para formar 10 unidades y sumarla a las unidades existentes. $$64 = \overset{50}{\cancel{60}} + \overset{14}{\cancel{4}}$$ $$-28 = 20 + 8$$ **Paso 3** Restar para hallar la respuesta. Los niños pueden restar de izquierda a derecha o de derecha a izquierda. $$64 = \overset{50}{\cancel{60}} + \overset{14}{\cancel{4}}$$ $$-28 = 20 + 8$$ $$\overline{30 + 6 = 36}$$	**Paso 1** Observar si hay suficientes unidades para restar. Si no las hay, desagrupar una de las 6 decenas en 64 para obtener 10 unidades. 4 unidades más las 10 unidades nuevas son 14 unidades. Dibujamos una lupa alrededor del número superior para ayudar a los niños a concentrarse en desagrupar. **Paso 2** Restar para hallar la respuesta. Los niños pueden restar de izquierda a derecha o de derecha a izquierda. 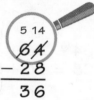

Cuando los niños expliquen el método que usan, deben hacerlo usando un lenguaje relacionado con "decenas y unidades". Esto demuestra que comprenden que están restando 2 decenas de 5 decenas (no 2 de 5) y 8 unidades de 14 unidades.

Si tiene alguna duda o algún comentario, por favor comuníquese conmigo.

Atentamente,
El maestro de su niño

CC SS En la Unidad 4 se aplican los siguientes estándares de los Estándares estatales comunes de matemáticas:
2.OA.A.1, 2.OA.B.2, 2.NBT.A.4, 2.NBT.B.5, 2.NBT.B.6, 2.NBT.B.7, 2.NBT.B.8, 2.NBT.B.9, 2.MD.C.8 y todos los de Prácticas matemáticas.

Name _____

Explain the Expanded Method

Mr. Green likes this method. Explain what he does.

Step 1	Step 2	Step 3
$64 = 60 + 4$ $- 28 = 20 + 8$	$\overset{50}{\cancel{6}}0 + \overset{14}{\cancel{4}}$ $64 = \cancel{60} + \cancel{4}$ $- 28 = 20 + 8$	$64 = \overset{50}{\cancel{60}} + \overset{14}{\cancel{4}}$ $- 28 = 20 + 8$ $30 + 6 = 36$

Try the Expanded Method

Show your work numerically and with a proof drawing.

1
$$\begin{array}{r} 42 \\ -\ 19 \\ \hline 23 \end{array}$$

2
$$\begin{array}{r} 75 \\ -\ 46 \\ \hline 38 \end{array}$$

3
$$\begin{array}{r} 81 \\ -\ 37 \\ \hline 56 \end{array}$$

Explain the Ungroup First Method

Mrs. Green likes this method. Explain what she does.

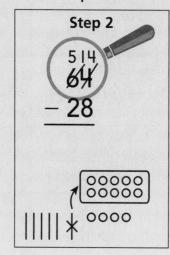

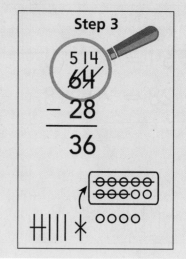

Step 1	Step 2	Step 3
64 − 28	5 14 6̶4̶ − 28	5 14 6̶4̶ − 28 36

Try the Ungroup First Method

Show your work numerically and with a proof drawing.

④ 42
  − 19

_____

⑤ 75
  − 46

_____

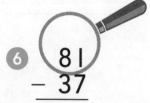

⑥ 81
  − 37

✓ Check Understanding

Describe two different ways to solve $46 - 17 = \square$.

Two Methods of Subtraction

PATH to FLUENCY **Subtract Within 100**

Subtract.

1) 65
   −16
   ——
    57

2) 58
   −37
   ——
    86

3) 20
   −14
   ——
    34

4) 74
   −23
   ——
    77

5) 19
   −17
   ——
    022

6) 50
   −13
   ——
    63

7) 87
   −30
   ——
   711

8) 91
   −45
   ——
    34

9) 31
   − 9
   ——
   310

10) 97
   −79
   ——

11) 20
   − 7
   ——

12) 46
   −36
   ——

Content Standards **2.NBT.B.5**
Mathematical Practices **MP1, MP2, MP5**

Fluency: Subtract

PATH to FLUENCY **Subtract Within 100** (continued)

Subtract.

⑬
$$\begin{array}{r} 100 \\ -\ 48 \\ \hline \end{array}$$
62

⑭
$$\begin{array}{r} 67 \\ -\ 31 \\ \hline \end{array}$$
36

⑮
$$\begin{array}{r} 55 \\ -\ 16 \\ \hline \end{array}$$
41

⑯
$$\begin{array}{r} 83 \\ -\ \ 8 \\ \hline \end{array}$$
75

⑰
$$\begin{array}{r} 40 \\ -\ 26 \\ \hline \end{array}$$
24

⑱
$$\begin{array}{r} 19 \\ -\ 11 \\ \hline \end{array}$$
8

⑲
$$\begin{array}{r} 14 \\ -\ 11 \\ \hline \end{array}$$
3

⑳
$$\begin{array}{r} 25 \\ -\ 12 \\ \hline \end{array}$$
13

㉑
$$\begin{array}{r} 100 \\ -\ 19 \\ \hline \end{array}$$
74

㉒
$$\begin{array}{r} 94 \\ -\ 76 \\ \hline \end{array}$$
12

㉓
$$\begin{array}{r} 20 \\ -\ \ 8 \\ \hline \end{array}$$
12

㉔
$$\begin{array}{r} 77 \\ -\ 24 \\ \hline \end{array}$$
13

✔ **Check Understanding**

Circle the correct answer to complete each sentence.

When subtracting 78 − 25, I _____ ungroup.   do / do not

When subtracting 78 − 29, I _____ ungroup.   do / do not

Fluency: Subtraction Within 100

Name _____ Date _____

Solve.   **Show your work.**

1
```
   92
 - 47
  68
```

2
```
  143
 - 81
```
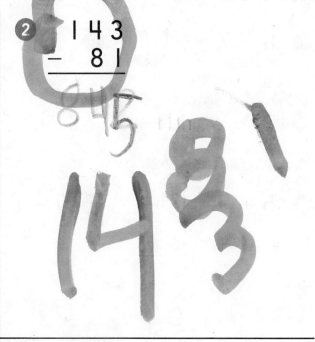
845

3
```
  126
 - 78
  167
```

4
```
  200
 - 79
  131
```

5 Kimberly has 94¢ in her pocket. She buys a can of
juice for 75¢. How much money does she have left?

_____

Name _____ Date _____

Add or subtract.

1 $8 - 7 = \boxed{1}$ **2** $13 - 5 = \boxed{8}$ **3** $9 - 3 = \boxed{6}$

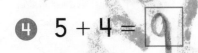

4 $5 + 4 = \boxed{9}$ **5** $7 + 5 = \boxed{12}$ **6** $8 + 8 = \boxed{16}$

7
$$\begin{array}{r} 47 \\ -15 \\ \hline 32 \end{array}$$

8
$$\begin{array}{r} 83 \\ -14 \\ \hline 71 \end{array}$$

9
$$\begin{array}{r} 56 \\ -42 \\ \hline 14 \end{array}$$

10
$$\begin{array}{r} 66 \\ +20 \\ \hline 86 \end{array}$$

11
$$\begin{array}{r} 31 \\ +14 \\ \hline 45 \end{array}$$

12
$$\begin{array}{r} 46 \\ +29 \\ \hline 75 \end{array}$$

13
$$\begin{array}{r} 88 \\ -59 \\ \hline \end{array}$$

14
$$\begin{array}{r} 91 \\ -67 \\ \hline \end{array}$$

15
$$\begin{array}{r} 100 \\ -36 \\ \hline \end{array}$$

Name _____

Addition and Subtraction Word Problems

Draw a Math Mountain to solve each word problem. Write an equation to match.

1 Teresa has 45 blocks. Then she finds 29 more blocks under the couch. How many blocks does Teresa have now?

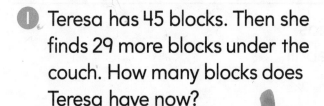

☐ _____
     label

2 The second grade art students make 163 masks. The art teacher displays 96 of the masks. How many masks are not displayed?

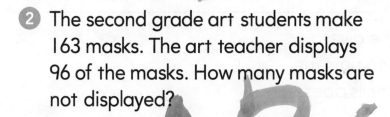

☐ _____
     label

3 There are 12 girls and 8 boys in the library. How many children are in the library altogether?

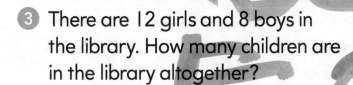

☐ _____
     label

4 There are 90 glue sticks in the school store. Then 52 glue sticks are sold. How many glue sticks are left?

☐ _____
     label

Addition and Subtraction Word Problems (continued)

Draw a Math Mountain to solve each word problem. Write an equation to match.

---

5 Sam has 47 baseball cards. Hank has 53 baseball cards. How many baseball cards do they have in all?

_____
label

---

6 Mrs. Snap has 42 pencils. She gives 29 pencils to her students and puts the rest in a box. How many pencils does she put in the box?

_____
label

---

7 At the park, Gabi collects 25 leaves. She collects 18 oak leaves, and the rest are maple leaves. How many are maple leaves?

_____
label

✔ Check Understanding

Explain how drawing a Math Mountain can help you decide whether to add or subtract to solve a word problem.

Word Problems with Addition and Subtraction

Name _____

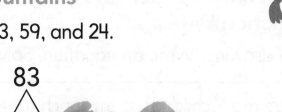

Find Equations for Math Mountains

1 Write all of the equations for 83, 59, and 24.

83

59   24

$59 + 24 = 83$ $83 = 59 + 24$

_____   _____

_____   _____

_____   _____

2 Write all of the equations for 142, 96, and 46.

142

96   46

$96 + 46 = 142$ $142 = 96 + 46$

_____   _____

_____   _____

_____   _____

Word Problem Practice: Addition and Subtraction Within 20

Make a drawing. Write an equation. Solve.

---

3 There are 7 children at the lunch table.
Some more children sit down.
Then there are 11 children at the table.
How many children sit down?

☐ _____
    label

---

4 Some leaves are on the ground. The children
pick up 9 leaves. Then there are 3 leaves on
the ground. How many leaves were on the
ground at the start?

☐ _____
    label

---

5 Stevie has 8 more stickers than Ari.
Stevie has 13 stickers. How many
stickers does Ari have?

☐ _____
    label

✓ **Check Understanding**

Draw and complete a Math Mountain with 100 at the
top and 45 on the bottom.

Equations with Greater Numbers

Name ___Hamza___

PATH to FLUENCY # Practice Addition and Subtraction Within 100

Add or subtract. Watch the sign!

1
$$91 - 63 = 32$$

2
$$36 + 9 = 44$$

3
$$100 - 74 = 36$$

4
$$45 + 39 = 54$$

5
$$64 - 23 = 43$$

6
$$33 + 66 = 99$$

7
$$20 - 4 = 19$$

8
$$34 + 38 = 70$$

9
$$52 - 38 = 26$$

10
$$43 + 57 = 100$$

11
$$96 - 78 = 34$$

12
$$13 + 79 = 94$$

CC SS Content Standards 2.OA.A.1, 2.NBT.A.1, 2.NBT.A.1.a, 2.NBT.B.5, 2.NBT.B.6, 2.NBT.B.7, 2.NBT.B.9 Mathematical Practices MP1, MP2, MP3, MP6

Practice Addition and Subtraction 231

Solve and Discuss

Solve each word problem.   Show your work.

13 Mr. Hepburn bakes 48 muffins on Monday. On
Tuesday, he bakes 24 muffins. How many muffins
does he bake during those two days?

```
┌──────┐
│      │  _____
└──────┘         label
```

14 Mrs. Jennings gets 75 new books for the class
library. She places 37 of them on the shelf. How
many new books are left to place on the shelf?

```
┌──────┐
│      │  _____
└──────┘         label
```

15 Usain has 64 toy cars. He puts 25 of the cars into
a box. How many cars are not in the box?

```
┌──────┐
│      │  _____
└──────┘         label
```

16 In June, Simone reads 18 books. In July,
she reads 35 books. How many books
does she read in June and July?

```
┌──────┐
│      │  _____
└──────┘         label
```

 Check Understanding

Write a subtraction equation to show the

solution for Problem 14. _____

Practice Addition and Subtraction

Name _____

Introduce the Juice Bar

Grapefruit Juice 11¢	Red Apple Juice 41¢ 	Lemon Juice 20¢ 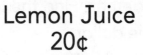	Pear Juice 22¢ 
Green Apple Juice 25¢	Peach Juice 40¢ 	Orange Juice 18¢ 	Cantaloupe Juice 10¢ 
Pineapple Juice 47¢ 	Raspberry Juice 33¢ 	Banana Juice 39¢	Watermelon Juice 15¢ 
Grape Juice 50¢ 	Celery Juice 36¢ 	Tomato Juice 30¢ 	Carrot Juice 29¢ 

CCSS Content Standards 2.NBT.B.5, 2.NBT.B.6, 2.MD.C.8
Mathematical Practices MP2, MP5

Buy and Sell with One Dollar **233**

Continue Buying and Selling

Choose two juice samples from the Juice Bar you would like to mix together. Find the total cost. Then find the change from one dollar.

1 I pick _____

and _____ .

Juice 1 price: _____ ¢

Juice 2 price: + _____ ¢

Total: _____

100¢ – _____ = _____

My change is _____ ¢.

2 I pick _____

and _____ .

Juice 1 price: _____ ¢

Juice 2 price: + _____ ¢

Total: _____

100¢ – _____ = _____

My change is _____ ¢.

3 I pick _____

and _____ .

Juice 1 price: _____ ¢

Juice 2 price: + _____ ¢

Total: _____

100¢ – _____ = _____

My change is _____ ¢.

4 I pick _____

and _____ .

Juice 1 price: _____ ¢

Juice 2 price: + _____ ¢

Total: _____

100¢ – _____ = _____

My change is _____ ¢.

 Check Understanding

Explain how to use the Adding Up Method to subtract 68¢ from $1.00.

Buy and Sell with One Dollar

Name _____

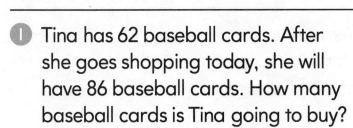

Practice the Adding Up Method

Add up to solve each word problem.   **Show your work.**

1 Tina has 62 baseball cards. After she goes shopping today, she will have 86 baseball cards. How many baseball cards is Tina going to buy?

☐ _____
label

2 Myra has 87 dollars. She buys some gifts. Then she has 68 dollars. How much money does Myra spend on gifts?

☐ _____
label

3 There are 15 apples in a basket. Some more apples are put in. Now there are 23 apples in the basket. How many apples are put in?

☐ _____
label

4 Ms. Baylon put 113 pebbles in the fish tank. Some of the pebbles are brown. 54 of the pebbles are black. How many pebbles are brown?

☐ _____
label

Practice the Adding Up Method (continued)

Add up to solve each word problem.   **Show your work.**

⑤ There are 25 bikes at a store. Then some
more bikes are brought to the store. Now there
are 48 bikes at the store. How many bikes are
brought to the store?

☐ _____
        label

⑥ There are 95 pieces of popcorn in a bag.
Sidney eats some of the pieces. Now there
are 52 pieces in the bag. How many pieces
does Sidney eat?

☐ _____
        label

⑦ In a package of stickers, there are
45 red stickers and some blue stickers.
There are 100 stickers in all. How many
stickers are blue?

☐ _____
        label

✓ **Check Understanding**

Choose a problem on this page. Make a
drawing to show how you used the Adding Up
Method to solve the problem.

Name _____

Practice the Adding Up Method

Add up to solve each word problem.   **Show your work.**

1. Last week, Justin read 27 comic books.
   Erika read some comic books too. In all,
   they read 86 comic books. How many
   comic books did Erika read?

   ⬜ _____
   label

2. In art class, the second grade boys and girls
   drew 73 pictures. The girls drew 38 of the
   pictures. How many pictures did the boys draw?

   ⬜ _____
   label

3. There are 82 birds in the zoo. The zoo gets
   some more birds. Now they have 100 birds.
   How many birds does the zoo get?

   ⬜ _____
   label

4. Mrs. Clark has 94 pens. She gives some
   pens to her friends. Now she has 75 pens.
   How many pens does Mrs. Clark give away?

   ⬜ _____
   label

CC SS Content Standards 2.OA.A.1, 2.NBT.B.5, 2.NBT.B.7, 2.NBT.B.9
Mathematical Practices MP1, MP6, MP7

Practice the Adding Up Method (continued)

Add up to solve each word problem.   **Show your work.**

5 Ike has 54 crayons. His sister gives him
some more crayons. Now he has 82 crayons.
How many crayons does his sister give him?

☐ _____
      label

6 In Mei's classroom, there are 39 books on a red shelf.
There are some books on a green shelf. There are
78 books on the two shelves. How many books are on
the green shelf?

☐ _____
      label

PATH to FLUENCY Add and Subtract Within 100

Add or subtract.

7   22
     + 30

8   17
     + 3

9   51
     + 34

10   86
      + 9

11 100
      − 68

12   92
      − 15

13   83
      − 77

14   54
      − 29

✓ **Check Understanding**

Look at Exercise 12. Add to check your work.
Make a drawing to show the addition.

More Word Problems with Unknown Addends

Name _____

Solve Complex Word Problems

Write an equation. Solve the problem.

1 Marian has a collection of toy cars. She gives 28 cars to her brother Simon. Marian has 57 cars left. How many cars did she have to begin with?

```
┌──────┐
│      │  _____
└──────┘
         label
```

2 In September, Mr. Shaw planted some tulip bulbs. In October, he planted 35 more bulbs. Altogether he planted 81 bulbs. How many bulbs did he plant in September?

```
┌──────┐
│      │  _____
└──────┘
         label
```

3 Mrs. Lyle has a collection of 19 caps. She buys some more. Now she has 34 caps. How many caps did Mrs. Lyle buy?

```
┌──────┐
│      │  _____
└──────┘
         label
```

4 Tarik picks 41 flowers. He gives some of the flowers to his aunt. He has 24 flowers left. How many flowers did Tarik give to his aunt?

```
┌──────┐
│      │  _____
└──────┘
         label
```

© Houghton Mifflin Harcourt Publishing Company

Solve Complex Word Problems (continued)

Write an equation. Solve the problem.

5 Frank has some markers. He buys 15 more markers. Now he has 62 markers. How many markers did Frank have to begin with?

[ ] _____
label

6 Kiki has 74 stickers. She gives some stickers to her friends. Now she has 29 stickers. How many stickers did Kiki give to her friends?

[ ] _____
label

7 Miss Harrod has a jar with some seeds in it. She gives 53 seeds to the science teacher. There are 37 seeds left in the jar. How many seeds were in the jar before?

[ ] _____
label

8 Josef has 59 sports cards. His friend Tara gives him some more cards. Now Josef has 78 sports cards. How many cards did Tara give him?

[ ] _____
label

 Check Understanding

Write a completed equation that starts with 27 and has 93 as the total.

_____

© Houghton Mifflin Harcourt Publishing Company

Start Unknown Problems

Name _____

Solve *Compare* Word Problems

Draw comparison bars and write an equation
to solve each problem.

1 Tia has 65 rocks. Stan has
29 rocks. How many more
rocks does Tia have than Stan?

```
┌──────┐ _____
│      │
└──────┘       label
```

2 Dora has 27 fewer grapes
than Jerry. Jerry has
72 grapes. How many
grapes does Dora have?

```
┌──────┐ _____
│      │
└──────┘       label
```

3 Lila has 34 toy trucks in her
collection, which is 18 fewer
than her friend Betty has.
How many toy trucks does
Betty have in her collection?

```
┌──────┐ _____
│      │
└──────┘       label
```

4 One year the Ricos planted
97 flowers. This was 29 more
flowers than the Smiths planted.
How many flowers did the
Smiths plant?

```
┌──────┐ _____
│      │
└──────┘       label
```

© Houghton Mifflin Harcourt Publishing Company

Solve *Compare* Word Problems (continued)

Draw comparison bars and write an equation to solve each problem.

5 Pippa has 48 more beads than Jeremy. Jeremy has 38 beads. How many beads does Pippa have?

[   ] _____
　　　　label

6 In the classroom, there are 25 fiction books and 64 nonfiction books. How many fewer fiction books than nonfiction books are in the classroom?

[   ] _____
　　　　label

7 Boris has 16 more cherries than Solongo. Boris has 60 cherries. How many cherries does Solongo have?

[   ] _____
　　　　label

✓ **Check Understanding**

Choose a problem from this page. Describe how you decided what label to use for the longer bar.

Compare Word Problems

Solve and Discuss

Make a drawing. Write an equation.
Solve.

1. Maxine's grandmother cuts out 48 fabric squares
to make a quilt. She needs 16 more squares to
complete the quilt. How many squares will be in
the quilt altogether?

   ☐ _____
   label

2. Mr. Adams buys 93 paper plates for a party.
He buys 43 large plates. The rest are small.
How many small plates does he buy?

   ☐ _____
   label

3. Henry collects shells. He has 32 shells. Jess gives him
some more shells. Now Henry has 51 shells. How
many shells did Jess give Henry?

   ☐ _____
   label

4. Trina's team scores 56 points at the basketball game.
This is 30 more points than the other team scores.
How many points does the other team score?

   ☐ _____
   label

Solve and Discuss (continued)

Make a drawing. Write an equation.
Solve.

5. Maura gives 19 trading cards to Jim. Now she has 24 trading cards. How many trading cards did Maura have to start?

☐ _____
label

6. Jamal has 63 toy cars. Luis has 24 fewer toy cars than Jamal. How many toy cars does Luis have?

☐ _____
label

7. Ms. Dow has some red balloons and some blue balloons. Altogether she has 46 balloons. How many balloons of each color could she have?

☐ _____ and ☐ _____
label   label

8. Jon has 71 stickers. Ken has 53 stickers. How many fewer stickers does Ken have than Jon?

☐ _____
label

© Houghton Mifflin Harcourt Publishing Company

Mixed Word Problems

Name _____

Solve and Discuss (continued)

Make a drawing. Write an equation.
Solve.

---

9 Zoe has 22 more color pencils than Angelo.
Angelo has 38 color pencils. How many color
pencils does Zoe have?

☐ _____
label

---

10 Nima is matching spoons and forks. She finds
36 spoons and 50 forks. How many more spoons
does Nima need to have the same number of
spoons as forks?

☐ _____
label

---

11 Kirsty has some shells. Then she finds 24 more
shells at the beach. Now Kirsty has 100 shells.
How many shells did she start with?

☐ _____
label

---

12 Landon has 84 beads. He uses some beads to
make a necklace. Now he has 45 beads left.
How many beads does Landon use to make
the necklace?

☐ _____
label

Mixed Word Problems **245**

What's the Error?

Sona has 63 balloons. That is 16 more balloons than Molly. How many balloons does Molly have?

$$63 + 16 = 79$$
Sona   more   Molly

Did I make a mistake?

13 Draw comparison bars to help Puzzled Penguin. Write an equation to solve the problem.

Molly has ☐ balloons.

PATH to FLUENCY Add and Subtract Within 100

Add or subtract.

14
$$\begin{array}{r} 34 \\ +46 \\ \hline \end{array}$$

15
$$\begin{array}{r} 13 \\ +78 \\ \hline \end{array}$$

16
$$\begin{array}{r} 49 \\ +26 \\ \hline \end{array}$$

17
$$\begin{array}{r} 95 \\ -38 \\ \hline \end{array}$$

18
$$\begin{array}{r} 61 \\ -28 \\ \hline \end{array}$$

19
$$\begin{array}{r} 60 \\ -33 \\ \hline \end{array}$$

✔ **Check Understanding**
Choose a problem from page 245. Explain how your drawing and equation match the problem.

Mixed Word Problems

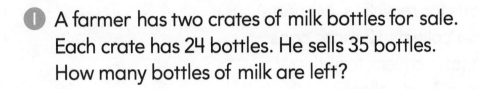

Solve Two-Step Problems

Think about the first-step question.
Then solve the problem.

---

1 A farmer has two crates of milk bottles for sale.
Each crate has 24 bottles. He sells 35 bottles.
How many bottles of milk are left?

☐ _____
label

---

2 There are 26 children at the library. 12 are girls and
the rest are boys. Then 7 more boys come to the
library. How many boys are at the library now?

☐ _____
label

---

3 Jeff has 2 boxes of crayons and 15 other
crayons. Each box contains 36 crayons.
How many crayons does Jeff have altogether?

☐ _____
label

Solve Two-Step Problems (continued)

Think about the first-step question.
Then solve the problem.

---

④ Lane collects 18 cans for recycling. Monette
collects 9 cans. Julia collects 12 more cans
than Lane and Monette collect together.
How many cans does Julia collect?

☐ _____
   label

---

⑤ Fiona has 17 action figures. Logan has 9 more
action figures than Fiona. Bonnie has 12 fewer
action figures than Logan. How many action
figures does Bonnie have?

☐ _____
   label

---

⑥ Mr. Tyson makes 75 rings to sell at a fair. He sells
16 rings on the first day. He sells some more on the
second day. Now he has 22 rings left. How many
rings did Mr. Tyson sell on the second day?

☐ _____
   label

 Check Understanding
Draw the problem situation from Problem 5.

© Houghton Mifflin Harcourt Publishing Company

Two-Step Problems

Solve Two-Step Problems

Think about the first-step question.
Then solve the problem.

---

1 Lin gets $38 for babysitting. She spends $12 on a present for her mother and puts the rest in a money jar. She then gives some money to her sister. Now Lin has $18 in her money jar. How many dollars did Lin give her sister?

☐ _____
label

---

2 Russell has 28 marbles. Ridge has 12 fewer marbles than Russell. Natasha has as many marbles as Russell and Ridge together. How many marbles does Natasha have?

☐ _____
label

---

3 Mr. Verdi is sewing costumes for the school play. He needs 26 blue buttons. He also needs 16 green buttons and 34 red buttons. How many buttons does Mr. Verdi need in all?

☐ _____
label

© Houghton Mifflin Harcourt Publishing Company

Solve Two-Step Problems (continued)

Think about the first-step question.
Then solve the problem.

4 Mrs. Glover is sorting 56 feathers by color. 25 feathers are red and the rest are green. Mrs. Glover adds some more green feathers. Now she has 36 green feathers. How many green feathers did Mrs. Glover add?

☐ _____
　　　　　label

5 Gabe and Juan find 32 leaves. Mari and Kaila find 12 more leaves than Gabe and Juan. If Mari finds 19 leaves, how many leaves does Kaila find?

☐ _____
　　　　　label

6 Kyle plants 15 seeds in the first pot. He plants 12 seeds in the second pot and 18 seeds in the third pot. The fourth pot is large. He plants as many seeds in the fourth pot as in all the other three pots. How many seeds does Kyle plant in the four pots altogether?

☐ _____
　　　　　label

✓ **Check Understanding**

Write the first-step question and answer for Problem 5.

_____

_____

　　　　　More Two-Step Problems

Name _____

Make Measurements

The Stegosaurus was a large plant-eating dinosaur.
It had two rows of plates running along its back
and long spikes on its tail.

The feet of the Stegosaurus were short and wide.
The forefeet (the feet on the front legs) had
five short, wide toes with short hoof-like
tips. The rear feet had three short,
wide toes with hooves.

1. The rear foot of a Stegosaurus was about
   35 centimeters long. Use scissors and tape to make
   a paper strip that is 35 centimeters long. Write on
   the strip: *Foot of Stegosaurus.*

2. Now measure your own foot in centimeters.

   My foot is ☐ centimeters long.

   Make a paper strip that is the same length as your
   foot. Write on the strip: *My Foot.*

3. How much longer is the foot of the Stegosaurus
   than your foot?

   ☐ centimeters

© Houghton Mifflin Harcourt Publishing Company

Content Standards **2.OA.A.1, 2.NBT.B.5, 2.NBT.B.7, 2.MD.A.1, 2.MD.A.3, 2.MD.A.4, 2.MD.B.5** Mathematical Practices **MP1, MP2, MP3, MP4, MP5, MP6**   Focus on Mathematical Practic

Measure Stride

4 Work with a partner to measure your *stride*.

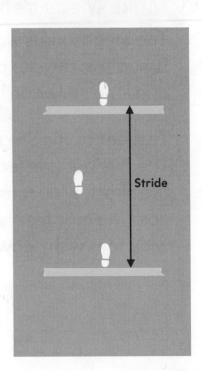

STEP 1. Put a piece of tape on the floor.

STEP 2. Line up your right and left heels with the edge of the tape.

STEP 3. Take a normal walking step with your left foot.

STEP 4. Take a normal walking step with your right foot.

STEP 5. Use tape to mark where the heel of your right foot lands.

STEP 6. Measure the distance in centimeters between the two pieces of tape. This is your *stride*.

My stride is ☐ centimeters long.

Make a paper strip that is the same length as your stride. Write on the strip: *My Stride*.

5 The stride of the Stegosaurus is measured using footprints from its right hind leg. Its stride was about 190 centimeters. Make a paper strip that is 190 centimeters long. Write on it: *Stride of Stegosaurus*.

6 How much longer is the stride of the Stegosaurus than your stride?

☐ centimeters

7 Compare your stride with your partner's stride.

Who has the longer stride? _____

How much longer is it? ☐ centimeters

Focus on Mathematical Practices

Name _____   Date _____

Solve.   Show your work.

1 Mrs. Rose buys 64 new pencils for her class. She sharpens 45 of them. How many pencils still need to be sharpened?

☐ _____
      label

2 Jill has 64 markers. Sam has 48 markers. How many more markers does Jill have than Sam?

☐ _____
      label

3 Jeff has a collection of baseball cards. He gives 36 baseball cards to his sister Clara. Jeff has 39 baseball cards left. How many baseball cards did he have at first?

☐ _____
      label

4 Clarissa has $1.00. She buys 2 pencils. Each pencil costs 45¢. How much change should Clarissa get?

_____

Name _____   Date _____

Add or subtract.

1 $7 + 9 = \boxed{16}$ **2** $9 + 6 = \boxed{15}$ **3** $13 + 5 = \boxed{18}$

4 $18 - 7 = \boxed{}$ **5** $13 - 5 = \boxed{}$ **6** $7 - 1 = \boxed{}$

7
$$\begin{array}{r} 24 \\ + 13 \\ \hline 38 \end{array}$$

8
$$\begin{array}{r} 39 \\ + 24 \\ \hline 59 \end{array}$$

9
$$\begin{array}{r} 67 \\ + 29 \\ \hline \end{array}$$

10
$$\begin{array}{r} 46 \\ - 9 \\ \hline \end{array}$$

11
$$\begin{array}{r} 50 \\ - 15 \\ \hline \end{array}$$

12
$$\begin{array}{r} 51 \\ - 38 \\ \hline \end{array}$$

13
$$\begin{array}{r} 94 \\ - 51 \\ \hline \end{array}$$

14
$$\begin{array}{r} 100 \\ - 88 \\ \hline \end{array}$$

15
$$\begin{array}{r} 91 \\ - 75 \\ \hline \end{array}$$

1 Subtract. Match each subtraction to its answer.

$$\begin{array}{r} 74 \\ -38 \\ \hline \end{array}$$ •   • 46

$$\begin{array}{r} 63 \\ -17 \\ \hline \end{array}$$ •   • 39

91 − 52 •   • 36

---

2 Is the answer correct? Choose Yes or No.

$$\begin{array}{r} 17 \\ -\ 4 \\ \hline 12 \end{array}$$ ○ Yes   ○ No

$$\begin{array}{r} 20 \\ -\ 9 \\ \hline 11 \end{array}$$ ○ Yes   ○ No

$$\begin{array}{r} 41 \\ -\ 7 \\ \hline 34 \end{array}$$ ○ Yes   ○ No

---

3 Hector has 1 dollar, 2 quarters, 1 dime, 3 nickels, and 1 penny.

Draw ☐100 s, ⊙25 s, ⊙10 s, ⊙5 s, ⊙1 s

Write the total amount of money. $ _____ . _____ _____

total

Under each picture, write the total amount of
money so far. Then write the total using $.

4   25¢   25¢   25¢   10¢   10¢   10¢

___25¢___   ___50¢___   _____   _____   _____   _____

$ _____ . _____ _____
                                    total

Subtract.

5   100
       − 63
     _____

6   108
       − 29
     _____

7 Write a subtraction problem to match the equation.
Make a proof drawing to solve the problem.

43 − 34 = ▧

□

Do you need to ungroup to subtract?
Choose Yes or No.

8 $\begin{array}{r} 1\,4\,0 \\ -\ \ 8\,9 \end{array}$

○ Yes   ○ No

$\begin{array}{r} 2\,0\,0 \\ -\ \ 5\,4 \end{array}$

○ Yes   ○ No

Solve.   Show your work.

9 Jaime, David, and Taylor have beads to make key chains. Jaime has 24 beads. David has 12 more beads than Jaime. Taylor has 14 fewer beads than David. How many beads does Taylor have?

[ ] _____
         label

10 Charlotte, Dustin, and Randy are picking peaches. Charlotte picks 14 peaches, Dustin picks 28 peaches, and Randy picks 23 peaches. How many peaches do they pick?

[ ] _____
         label

11 There are 27 marbles in a bag. Kim puts more marbles into the bag. Now there are 59 marbles in the bag. How many marbles does Kim put into the bag?

[ ] _____
         label

12 Brad subtracts 65 from 151. Should he follow the steps listed below? Choose Yes or No.

Ungroup 5 tens as 4 tens 10 ones.	○ Yes	○ No
Subtract 5 ones from 10 ones.	○ Yes	○ No
Subtract 6 tens from 4 tens.	○ Yes	○ No
Subtract 6 tens from 14 tens.	○ Yes	○ No

13 Jeff wants to buy a baseball card for $1.52. Show two ways he could pay for the baseball card.

☐ dollars ☐ quarters ☐ dimes

☐ nickels ☐ pennies

☐ dollars ☐ quarters ☐ dimes

☐ nickels ☐ pennies

14 Subtract 38 from 57. Explain all the steps you use.

```
  5 7
- 3 8
```

Name _____

The Fruit Stand

1 You have 2 quarters, 2 dimes, and 1 nickel.
Ring one fruit that you could buy from the fruit stand.

   56¢   47¢   83¢   39¢

Show the method you used to get the answer.

2 Draw coins to show the money you have left.
Use as few coins as possible.

3 Which fruit should you buy to have the greatest
amount of money left? Explain.

_____

_____

_____

Name _____

Solve.

4 Nina has 8 dimes. She buys an apple. Does she have enough money left to buy a banana? Explain.

5 Camilla has 1 dollar, 2 quarters, and 3 dimes. Can she buy two pears and an apple? Explain.

6 Jacob has 3 dimes and 5 nickels. Cassie has 5 dimes and 3 nickels. Who has enough money to buy an apple? Explain.

Dear Family:

Your child is beginning a new unit on time.

You can help your child link the time concepts learned in school with the real world.

Together, look for clocks in your home. You might search for watches, alarm clocks, digital clocks, and clocks on appliances.

Talk about time throughout your family's day. For example, you can point to the clock during breakfast and say, "We usually eat breakfast at this time. It is 7:30 A.M."

In this unit, your child will learn to tell time to the hour, half hour, and five minutes. Your child will practice writing the time.

If you have any questions or comments, please contact me. Thank you.

Sincerely,
Your child's teacher

Unit 5 addresses the following standards from the Common Core State Standards for Mathematics: **2.OA.A.1, 2.OA.B.2, 2.NBT.A.2, 2.NBT.A.4, 2.NBT.B.5, 2.MD.C.7, 2.MD.D.10, 2.G.A.3, and all** Mathematical Practices.

Estimada familia:

Su niño está empezando una unidad donde aprenderá sobre la hora.

Usted puede ayudarlo a que conecte los conceptos relacionados con la hora que aprendió en la escuela, con el mundo real.

Busquen juntos relojes en la casa. Puede buscar relojes de pulsera, relojes con alarma, relojes digitales y relojes que estén en los electrodomésticos.

Durante un día en familia, hablen de la hora. Por ejemplo, puede señalar un reloj durante el desayuno y decir: "Generalmente desayunamos a esta hora. Son las 7:30 a.m."

En esta unidad su niño aprenderá a leer la hora en punto, la media hora y los cinco minutos para la hora. Su niño practicará cómo escribir la hora.

Si tiene alguna pregunta o algún comentario, por favor comuníquese conmigo. Gracias.

Atentamente,
El maestro de su niño

© Houghton Mifflin Harcourt Publishing Company

CC SS **En la Unidad 5 se aplican los siguientes estándares de los** Estándares estatales comunes de matemáticas: **2.OA.A.1, 2.OA.B.2, 2.NBT.A.2, 2.NBT.A.4, 2.NBT.B.5, 2.MD.C.7, 2.MD.D.10, 2.G.A.3 y todos los de** Prácticas matemáticas.

A.M.

clock

analog clock

data

bar graph

digital clock

analog
clock

digital
clock

Use A.M. for times between midnight and noon.

	Sisters	Brothers
Kendra	2	1
Scott	2	0
Ida	0	1

← data

The data in the table show how many sisters and how many brothers each child has.

horizontal bar graph

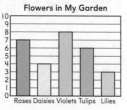

vertical bar graph

horizontal
bar graph

picture graph

hour hand

P.M.

minute hand

survey

Apples	🍎🍎🍎🍎🍎🍎🍎
Oranges	⚫⚫⚫⚫⚫⚫⚫⚫⚫

Use P.M. for times between noon and midnight.

hour hand

When you collect data by asking people questions, you are taking a survey.

minute hand: points to the minutes

vertical bar
graph

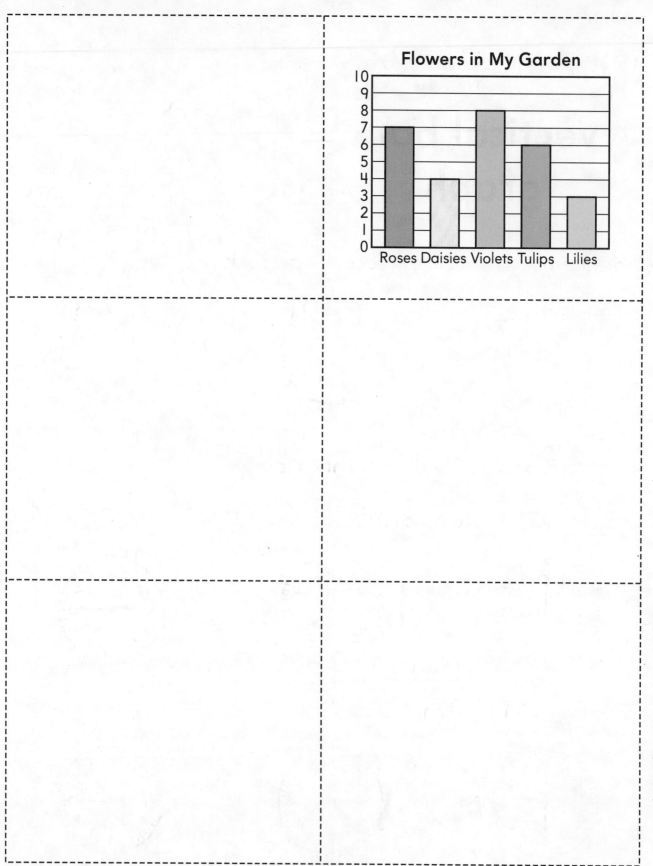

Flowers in My Garden

Roses	Daisies	Violets	Tulips	Lilies

Name _____

VOCABULARY
clock
analog clock
minute hand
hour hand

Features of Clocks

A **clock** is a tool that we use to measure time.

1 Describe some clocks that you have seen.

_____

_____

_____

Write the missing numbers on each **analog clock**.

2

3

4

An analog clock has a long hand that is the **minute hand** and a short hand that is the **hour hand**.
Circle the hour hand on each clock.

5

6

7

Circle the minute hand on each clock.

8

9

10

Times of Daily Activities

VOCABULARY

A.M.

P.M.

We use A.M. for the hours after 12:00 midnight and before 12:00 noon.
9:00 A.M. is 9 o'clock in the morning.
We use P.M. for the hours after 12:00 noon and before 12:00 midnight.
9:00 P.M. is 9 o'clock in the evening.

11 Complete the chart. For each time listed, write whether it is dark or light outside; whether it is morning, afternoon, or evening; and an activity you might be doing at that time.

Time	Sunlight	Part of the Day	Activity
4:00 A.M.	dark	morning	sleeping
12:30 P.M.			
9:00 P.M.			

For each activity, circle the most appropriate time.

12 brush your teeth in the morning

1:30 P.M.   3:00 P.M.   7:30 A.M.

13 eat dinner at night

5:00 A.M.   12:00 noon   6:00 P.M.

14 watch an afternoon movie

3:00 A.M.   2:00 P.M.   6:00 P.M.

Hours and A.M. or P.M.

Name _____

Model a Clock

Attach the clock hands using a prong fastener.

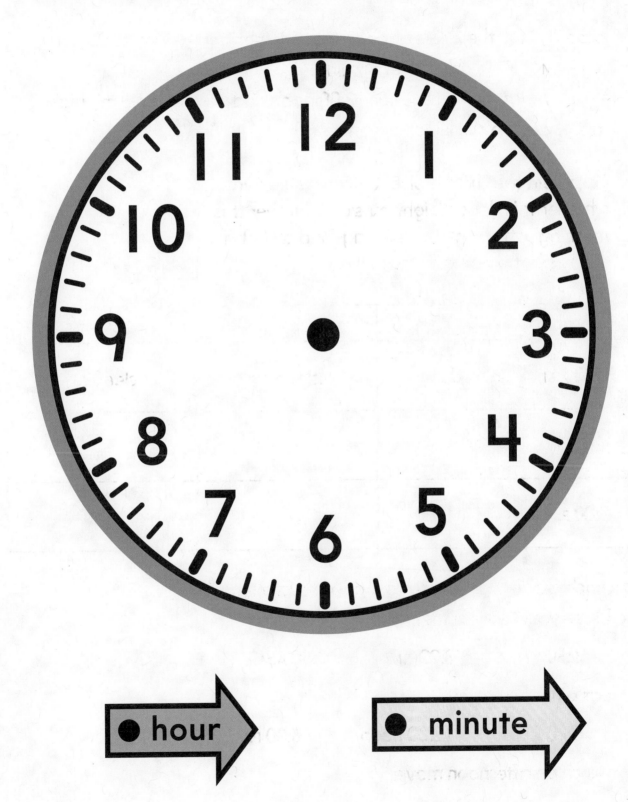

Paper Clock

Name _____

Write Time

On a **digital clock**, the number on the left shows the hour, and the number on the right shows the minutes after the hour.

hour   minutes

Write the time in two different ways.

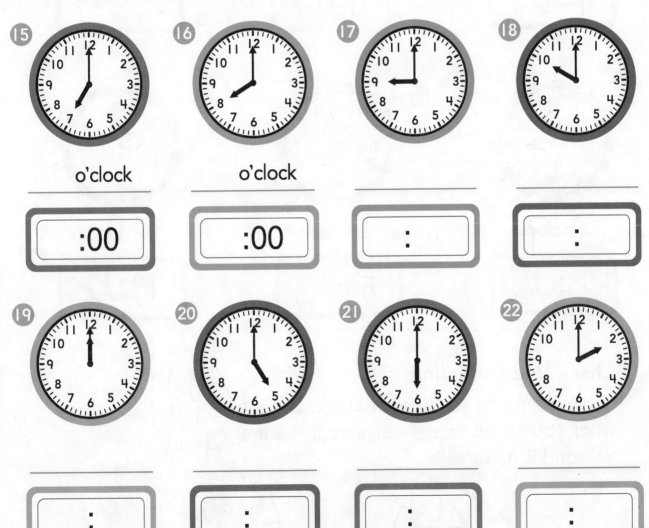

15

o'clock

:00

16

o'clock

:00

17

:

18

:

19

:

20

:

21

:

22

:

© Houghton Mifflin Harcourt Publishing Company

Draw Clock Hands

Draw the hands on each analog clock, and write
the time on each digital clock below.

7 o'clock

11 o'clock

2 o'clock

3 o'clock

5 o'clock

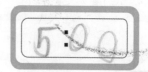

10 o'clock

✓ Check Understanding

Show a time on your paper clock. Describe
what you would do at that time if it were
A.M. and if it were P.M.

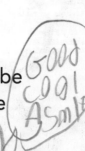

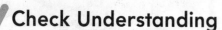

Hours and A.M. or P.M.

Name _Hamza_

5-Minute Intervals

1. Count by 5s around the clock.

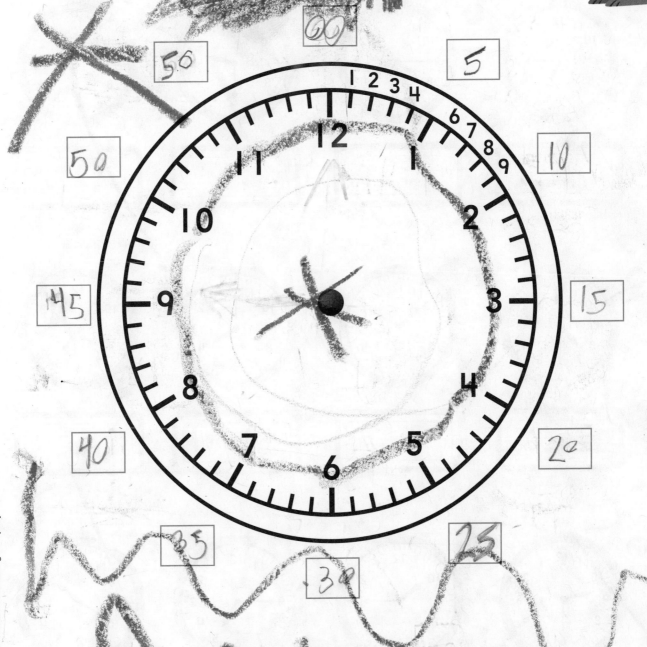

55 | 60 | 5

50 | | 10

45 | | 15

40 | | 20

35 | 30 | 25

Read Time to 5 Minutes

Write the time on the digital clock.

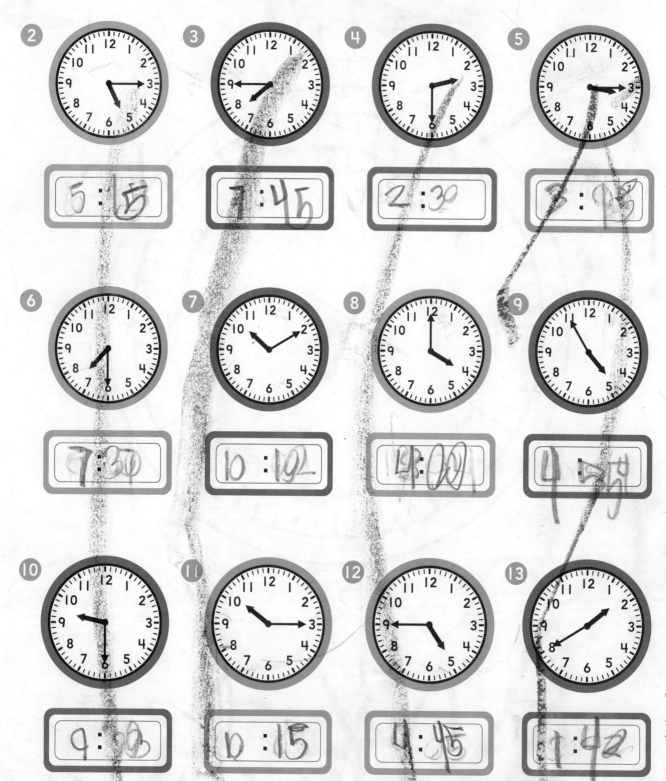

2. 5:15

3. 7:45

4. 2:30

5. 3:15

6. 7:30

7. 10:12

8. 4:00

9. 4:35

10. 9:03

11. 10:15

12. 4:45

13. 1:42

Hours and Minutes

Name _____

Show Time to 5 Minutes

Draw hands on each clock to show the time.

⑭

`10:35`

⑮

`9:20`

⑯

`2:25`

⑰

`4:50`

⑱

`7:05`

⑲

`3:30`

⑳

`5:50`

㉑

`8:00`

㉒

`10:15`

㉓

`12:25`

㉔

`3:55`

㉕

`4:30`

What's the Error?

5:55

Did I make a mistake?

26 What is the correct time?

5 : 11

A.M. or P.M.?

For each activity, circle the appropriate time.

27 picnic

5:30 A.M.
5:30 P.M.

28 school recess

10:00 A.M.
10:00 P.M.

29 afternoon snack

3:15 A.M.
3:15 P.M.

30 going to the playground

9:25 A.M.
9:25 P.M.

31 lunch

12:10 A.M.
12:10 P.M.

32 sunset

7:05 A.M.
7:05 P.M.

33 wake up

6:45 A.M.
6:45 P.M.

34 math class

8:30 A.M.
8:30 P.M.

✓ Check Understanding

At 6:25, where does the minute hand point?

1 For the activity, circle the time that makes sense.

eat dinner

 A.M.    P.M.

Write the time on the digital clock.

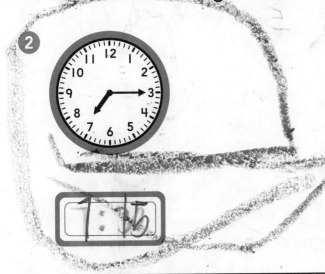

2

3

Draw hands on the clock to show the time.

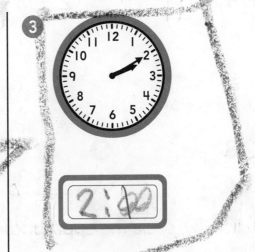

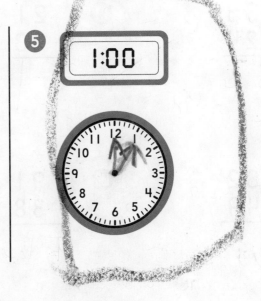

4 6:05

5 1:00

Name _Hanza_   Date _4/17/8_

PATH to
FLUENCY

Add or subtract.

1 $9 + 7 = \boxed{15}$ **2** $15 - 5 = \boxed{20}$ **3** $7 - 3 = \boxed{16}$

4 $7 + 4 = \boxed{11}$ **5** $2 + 3 = \boxed{5}$ **6** $6 + 8 = \boxed{14}$

7
$$\begin{array}{r} 28 \\ -17 \\ \hline 116 \end{array}$$

8
$$\begin{array}{r} 78 \\ -58 \\ \hline 28 \end{array}$$

9
$$\begin{array}{r} 47 \\ -31 \\ \hline 19 \end{array}$$

10
$$\begin{array}{r} 33 \\ +24 \\ \hline 57 \end{array}$$

11
$$\begin{array}{r} 21 \\ +13 \\ \hline 34 \end{array}$$

12
$$\begin{array}{r} 26 \\ +46 \\ \hline 63 \end{array}$$

13
$$\begin{array}{r} 82 \\ -49 \\ \hline 33 \end{array}$$

14
$$\begin{array}{r} 91 \\ -38 \\ \hline 593 \end{array}$$

15
$$\begin{array}{r} 100 \\ -71 \\ \hline 29 \end{array}$$

Dear Family:

Your child is learning how to show information in various ways. In this unit, children will learn how to create and read picture graphs and bar graphs.

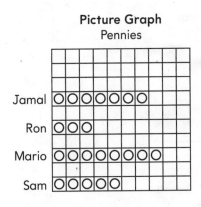

Picture Graph
Pennies

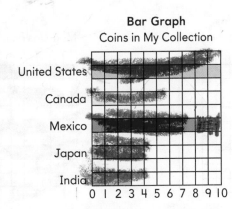

Bar Graph
Coins in My Collection

An important feature of *Math Expressions* is its emphasis on real world connections. Children will collect and represent data on graphs. They will also interpret the graph to answer questions about the data shown.

Children also explore the language of comparison by using such words as *same, more, less,* and *fewer.* The connection between pairs of terms is emphasized. For example: Carlos has 8 stickers. Maria has 3. Carlos has 5 *more* stickers than Maria. Maria has 5 *fewer* stickers than Carlos has.

Please call if you have any questions or concerns. Thank you for helping your child learn how to create, read, and interpret graphs.

Sincerely,
Your child's teacher

CC SS Unit 5 addresses the following standards from the Common Core State Standards for Mathematics: **2.OA.A.1, 2.OA.B.2, 2.NBT.A.2, 2.NBT.A.4, 2.NBT.B.5, 2.MD.C.7, 2.MD.D.10, 2.G.A.3,** and all Mathematical Practices.

Estimada familia:

Su niño está aprendiendo a mostrar información de varias maneras. En esta unidad los niños aprenderán a crear y a leer gráficas de dibujos y gráficas de barras.

Gráfica de dibujos
Monedas de 1 centavo

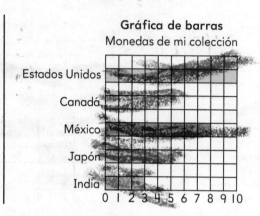

Gráfica de barras
Monedas de mi colección

Un aspecto importante de *Math Expressions* es su énfasis en las conexiones con situaciones de la vida cotidiana. Los niños reunirán datos y los representarán en gráficas. También interpretarán las gráficas para responder preguntas acerca de los datos que se muestran.

Los niños también estudiarán palabras que se usan para comparar, tales como *igual, mismo, más* y *menos*. Se hará énfasis en la conexión entre los pares de términos. Por ejemplo: Carlos tiene 8 adhesivos. María tiene 3. Carlos tiene 5 adhesivos *más* que María. María tiene 5 adhesivos *menos* que Carlos.

Si tiene alguna pregunta o algún comentario, por favor comuníquese conmigo. Gracias por ayudar a su niño a aprender cómo crear, leer e interpretar gráficas.

Atentamente,
El maestro de su niño

© Houghton Mifflin Harcourt Publishing Company

Name ___Hamza___ 4/18/18

Read to Make a Horizontal Picture Graph

Read the sentences below. Use the information
to make a horizontal picture graph.

Number of stickers

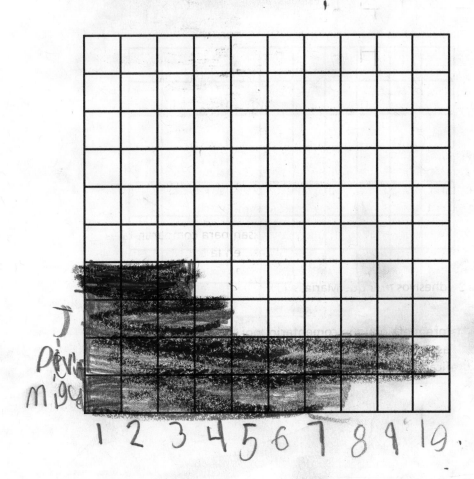

1 2 3 4 5 6 7 8 9 10

1 Miguel has 6 stickers.

2 Devin has 8 stickers.

3 Jennie has 4 stickers.

4 Hank has 3 stickers.

Read to Make a Vertical Picture Graph

Read the sentences below. Use the information
to make a vertical picture graph.

Number of comxbook

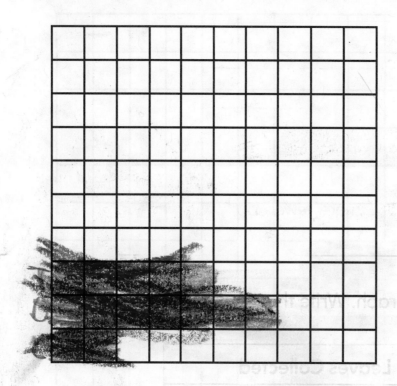

5 Carly has 2 comic books.

6 Dayo has 7 comic books.

7 Tomas has 5 comic books.

✔ Check Understanding

Shanice has 2 more comic books than Dayo. Add this
information to the vertical picture graph.

Discuss Picture Graphs

Name _____

Use Picture Graphs to Compare Amounts

Read the **picture graph**.

Write the number. Circle *more* or *fewer*.

Number of Balloons	
Carla	🎈🎈🎈🎈🎈🎈🎈
Peter	🎈🎈🎈🎈
Hanna	🎈🎈🎈🎈🎈

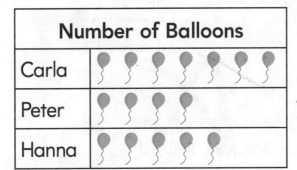

1. Carla has [ ] *more* *fewer* balloons than Peter.

2. Hanna has [ ] *more* (*fewer*) balloons than Carla.

Read the picture graph. Write the number.

Leaves Collected	
Amari	🍂🍂🍂🍂
Sam	🍂🍂🍂🍂🍂🍂🍂🍂
Marco	🍂🍂🍂🍂🍂🍂

3. Amari needs [4] more leaves to have as many as Sam has.

4. If Sam gives away [2] leaves, he will have as many leaves as Marco has.

Solve *Put Together/Take Apart* Problems

This picture graph shows the number of apples Mrs. Reid bought at the store.

Apples Bought				
Red	🍎	🍎	🍎	🍎
Green	🍏	🍏		
Yellow	🍏	🍏		

5 How many apples did Mrs. Reid buy?

8	apples

　　　　label

6 There are 2 green apples, 1 yellow apple, and 1 red apple in the bowl. The rest are in Mrs. Reid's bag. How many apples are in the bag?

4	applesinthebag

　　　　label

This picture graph shows the number of books that four children read.

Books Read				
Pablo	📘	📘	📘	
Janis	📘	📘		
Helen	📘			
Ray	📘	📘	📘	📘

7 Two children read 6 books altogether. Who are the two children?

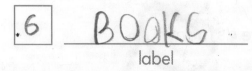

Janis and Rey

8 Two of the books the children read are about cars and 2 books are about trains. The rest of the books are about animals. How many books are about animals?

.6	Books

　　　　label

✔ **Check Understanding**

How many more books would Janis need to read to equal the number of books Pablo and Ray read altogether? _____

Read Picture Graphs

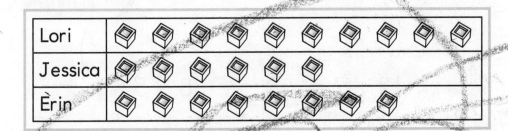

Lori	🔲 🔲 🔲 🔲 🔲 🔲 🔲 🔲 🔲 🔲
Jessica	🔲 🔲 🔲 🔲 🔲 🔲
Erin	🔲 🔲 🔲 🔲 🔲 🔲 🔲 🔲

Use the picture graph. Write the number.
Ring **more** or **fewer**.

1 Erin has ⟨8⟩ **more fewer** blocks than Jessica.

2 Jessica has ⟨6⟩ **more fewer** blocks than Lori.

3 Lori has ⟨10⟩ **more fewer** blocks than Erin.

Matthew	🐚 🐚 🐚 🐚 🐚
Cayden	🐚 🐚 🐚 🐚 🐚 🐚 🐚 🐚 🐚
John	🐚 🐚 🐚 🐚 🐚 🐚 🐚 🐚

Use the picture graph. Write the number.
Ring **more** or **fewer**.

4 Matthew has ⟨5⟩ **more fewer** shells than Cayden.

5 Cayden has ⟨9⟩ **more fewer** shells than John.

Name _____   Date _____

Add or subtract.

1 $5 + 3 =$ **8**   **2** $12 + 7 =$ **19**   **3** $8 + 5 =$ **13**

4 $12 - 4 =$ **16**   **5** $15 - 5 =$ **20**   **6** $15 - 9 =$ **24**

7
$$\begin{array}{r} 30 \\ +10 \\ \hline 40 \end{array}$$

8
$$\begin{array}{r} 41 \\ +27 \\ \hline 68 \end{array}$$

9
$$\begin{array}{r} 42 \\ +14 \\ \hline 56 \end{array}$$

10
$$\begin{array}{r} 54 \\ -12 \\ \hline \end{array}$$

11
$$\begin{array}{r} 38 \\ -20 \\ \hline \end{array}$$

12
$$\begin{array}{r} 67 \\ -39 \\ \hline \end{array}$$

13
$$\begin{array}{r} 24 \\ +58 \\ \hline 71 \end{array}$$

14
$$\begin{array}{r} 46 \\ +49 \\ \hline 81 \end{array}$$

15
$$\begin{array}{r} 74 \\ +26 \\ \hline 91 \end{array}$$

Name _____

Make a Picture Graph

Title: the NumBer toys

| Hamza |
| carlos |
| cainden |
| Jariel |

Hamza had the

Make a Bar Graph

Title: theNumBerFood

| Hamza |
| Hasan |
| Jheen |
| Zahr |

PATH to FLUENCY **Add and Subtract Within 100**

Add.

1 $46 + 4 = 50$ **2** $3 + 39 = 42$ **3** $26 + 71 = 97$

4
$$\begin{array}{r} 56 \\ +36 \\ \hline 92 \end{array}$$

5
$$\begin{array}{r} 11 \\ +47 \\ \hline 58 \end{array}$$

6
$$\begin{array}{r} 36 \\ +53 \\ \hline 89 \end{array}$$

7
$$\begin{array}{r} 78 \\ + 6 \\ \hline 84 \end{array}$$

8
$$\begin{array}{r} 25 \\ +61 \\ \hline 86 \end{array}$$

9
$$\begin{array}{r} 18 \\ +60 \\ \hline 78 \end{array}$$

10
$$\begin{array}{r} 44 \\ +17 \\ \hline 61 \end{array}$$

11
$$\begin{array}{r} 13 \\ + 5 \\ \hline 18 \end{array}$$

Subtract.

12 $74 - 8 = 66$ **13** $51 - 12 = 39$ **14** $60 - 15 = 55$

15
$$\begin{array}{r} 42 \\ -34 \\ \hline 18 \end{array}$$

16
$$\begin{array}{r} 78 \\ -29 \\ \hline 51 \end{array}$$

17
$$\begin{array}{r} 43 \\ -28 \\ \hline 15 \end{array}$$

18
$$\begin{array}{r} 50 \\ -18 \\ \hline 32 \end{array}$$

19
$$\begin{array}{r} 80 \\ -37 \\ \hline 43 \end{array}$$

20
$$\begin{array}{r} 64 \\ -45 \\ \hline 19 \end{array}$$

21
$$\begin{array}{r} 28 \\ -14 \\ \hline 14 \end{array}$$

22
$$\begin{array}{r} 56 \\ -27 \\ \hline 29 \end{array}$$

✓ **Check Understanding**

Describe how bar graphs are different from picture graphs.

Introduce Bar Graphs

Name _____

Read a Horizontal Bar Graph

Coins in My Collection

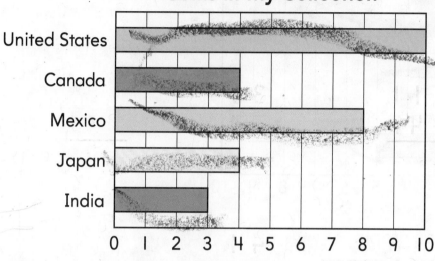

	0 1 2 3 4 5 6 7 8 9 10
United States	
Canada	
Mexico	
Japan	
India	

Read a Vertical Bar Graph

Flowers in My Garden

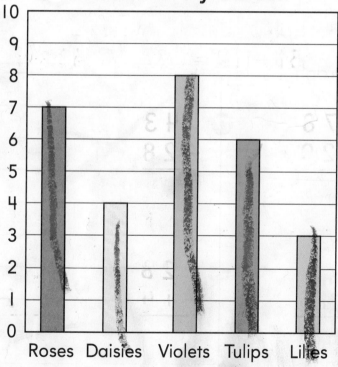

Roses Daisies Violets Tulips Lilies

Content Standards 2.OA.A.1, 2.MD.D.10
Mathematical Practices MP1, MP3, MP6, MP7

Write Comparison Statements

Awards We Earned

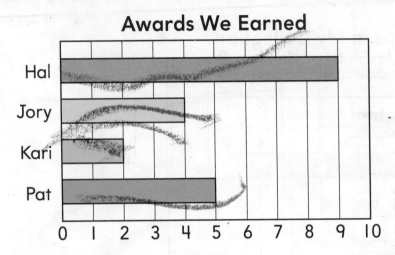

1 Use the horizontal bar graph.
Write an *is greater than* statement.

Make a Vertical Bar Graph

2 Make a vertical bar graph
from the horizontal
bar graph above.

✓ **Check Understanding**
Use the graph to write a
comparison problem on
your MathBoard. Trade
problems with a partner
and solve.

Read Bar Graphs

Name _____

Solve *Put Together/Take Apart* and *Compare* Problems

Animals at the Wildlife Park

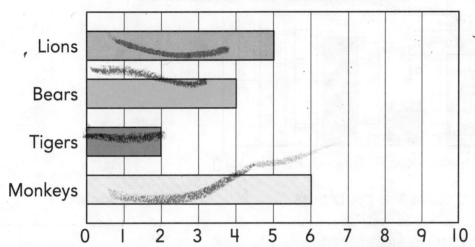

0   1   2   3   4   5   6   7   8   9   10

Use the bar graph to solve the problems.   **Show your work.**

---

1 Four of the monkeys are adults and the rest are babies. How many of the monkeys are babies?

2   monkeys $6 - 4 = 2$
    label

---

2 How many fewer bears are there than monkeys?

2   Bears $6 - 4 = 2$
    label

---

3 There are 2 fewer lions than elephants. How many elephants are there?

7   elephants
    label

© Houghton Mifflin Harcourt Publishing Company

Solve Word Problems with More Than One Step

Jenny's Bead Collection

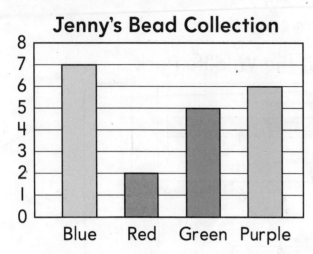

Use the bar graph to solve the problems.

Show your work.

---

4 Jenny has 4 fewer purple beads than Morgan. How many purple beads do Jenny and Morgan have in all?

label

---

5 Morgan has 11 red beads. Then she gives 2 red beads to Arun. How many more red beads does Morgan have now than Jenny?

label

---

6 Five of Jenny's beads are large and the rest are small. She buys some small yellow beads. Now she has 18 small beads. How many small yellow beads does she buy?

12 B Smileeds

label

Solve Problems Using a Bar Graph

Name _____

What's the Error?

Children's Favorite Snacks

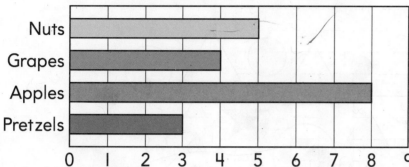

How many more children
choose fruit than nuts?

Fruit | 8 |
Nuts | 5 | ?

$$8 - 5 = 3$$

3 more children

Am I correct?

7 Show Puzzled Penguin how you
would solve the problem.

[ ] more children

Solve Problems Using a Bar Graph **289**

Organize and Graph Information

Here are some shapes for you to graph.

8 First make a table.   Then make a bar graph.

	Number

✓ **Check Understanding**
Explain another way
that you could sort and
graph the shapes. How
many shapes would be
in each group?

Solve Problems Using a Bar Graph

Name _____

VOCABULARY
survey
data

Record the Collected Data

1 Show the results of your **survey** in the table.
Your teacher will help you.

_____

_____	Number of Children

2 Show the **data** on a picture graph.

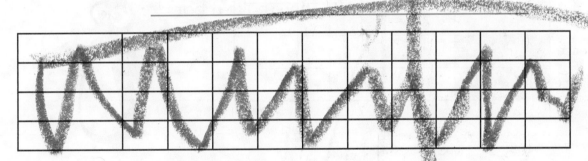

3 Show the data on a bar graph.

4 Use the data to write a 2-step word problem.

_____

_____

_____

CC SS Content Standards **2.MD.D.10**
Mathematical Practices **MP1, MP3, MP4, MP6**

What's the Error?

Favorite Subject	Number of Children
Reading	6
Math	7
Science	4
Art	4

Puzzled Penguin made a graph from the table.

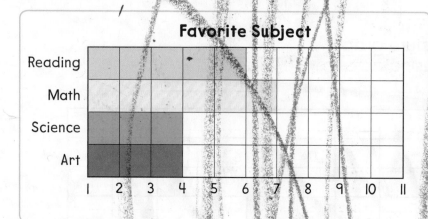

Favorite Subject

5 Fix Puzzled Penguin's errors.

PATH to FLUENCY Add and Subtract Within 100

Add or subtract.

6
$$\begin{array}{r} 7\,6 \\ +\,1\,7 \\ \hline \end{array}$$

7
$$\begin{array}{r} 6\,0 \\ -\,3\,7 \\ \hline \end{array}$$

8
$$\begin{array}{r} 1\,2 \\ +\,5\,1 \\ \hline \end{array}$$

9
$$\begin{array}{r} 4\,6 \\ -\,1\,9 \\ \hline \end{array}$$

 Check Understanding
When you take a survey, what are you doing?

_____

_____

Collect and Graph Data

Name _____

Make Graphs Using Data from a Table

The table shows the number of bicycles sold at a store on four days last week.

Bicycle Sales

Day	Number Sold
Saturday	8
Sunday	9
Monday	3
Tuesday	4

1. Make a picture graph using data from the table.

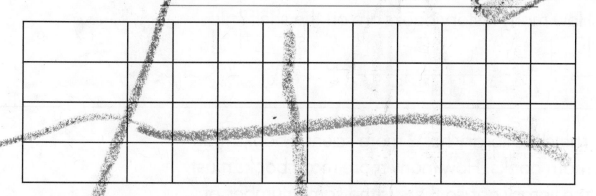

2. Make a bar graph using data from the table.

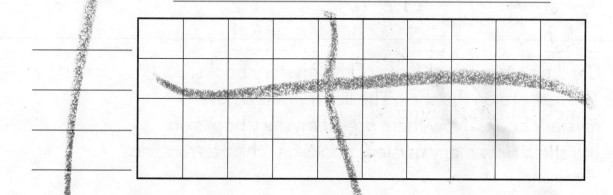

Solve Problems Using a Bar Graph

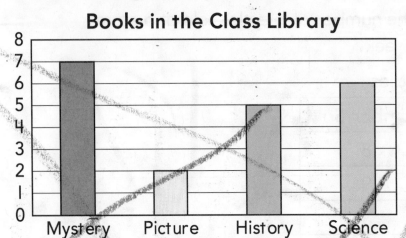

Books in the Class Library

Use the bar graph to solve the problems.   Show your work.

3 Children are reading 3 history books.
The rest are on the shelf in the library.
How many history books are on the shelf?

    □ _____
          label

4 The class library has 2 more science books than
math books. How many more math books must
the library get so there is the same number of
math books as mystery books?

    □ _____
          label

5 Children are reading some of the mystery books.
The rest are on the shelf. The library gets 6 new
mystery books. Now there are 10 mystery books on
the shelf. How many mystery books are children reading?

    □ _____
          label

Make Graphs and Interpret Data

© Houghton Mifflin Harcourt Publishing Company

Name _____

Solve Problems Using a Bar Graph (continued)

Animals at a Farm

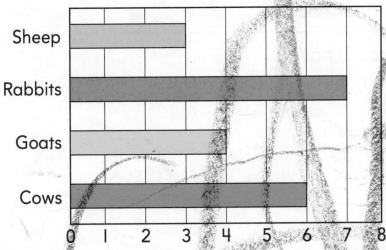

Use the bar graph to solve the problems.

Show your work.

6 The farm has 4 more rabbits than horses. How many horses does the farm have?

☐ _____
label

7 The farm has 5 fewer goats than chickens. How many chickens does the farm have?

☐ _____
label

8 There are 3 cows in the barn. The rest of the cows are in the field with the goats and the sheep. How many animals are in the field?

☐ _____
label

Make Graphs and Interpret Data **295**

Solve *Compare* Problems with 2-Digit Numbers

Solve. Draw comparison bars for each.

9 A park has 46 maple trees. It has 18 fewer elm trees. How many elm trees are in the park?

[   ] _____
         label

10 There are 62 pine trees in the park. There are 13 fewer pine trees than birch trees. How many birch trees are in the park?

[   ] _____
         label

11 The park has 27 fir trees. There are 16 more spruce trees than fir trees. The park has 28 fewer spruce trees than oak trees. How many oak trees are in the park?

[   ] _____
         label

✓ **Check Understanding**

Look at Problem 9. How many maple trees and elm trees are in the park altogether?

Make Graphs and Interpret Data

Name _____

Make a Graph

Mrs. Pratt asks the children in her class to tell which kitten they think is the cutest of these four kittens.

Fluffy   **Mink**   **Odin**   **Simba**

The results of the survey are shown in this table.

Which Kitten Do You Think Is the Cutest?

Fluffy	○○○○○ ○	6
Mink	○○○○	4
Odin	○○○○○ ○○○○	9
Simba	○○○○○ ○	6

1 Use the information in the table to make a bar graph.

_____

___ ___ ___ ___ ___ ___ ___ ___ ___ ___

Take a Survey

Your teacher will ask all of the children in the class to tell which puppy they think is the cutest of these four puppies.

Romy   Parker   Domino   Bernie

Show the results of the survey in this table.

Which Puppy Do You Think Is the Cutest?

Romy		
Parker		
Domino		
Bernie		

② Use the information in the table to make a bar graph on your MathBoard.

③ Write a 2-step word problem that can be solved by using the graph. Trade problems with a classmate. Solve each other's problems.

_____

_____

_____

Focus on Mathematical Practices

Name Hamza   Date 4/30/18

Use the picture graph.

1

Favorite Season

Winter	☺ ☺ ☺ ☺ ☺ ☺ ☺
Spring	☺ ☺ ☺ ☺
Summer	☺ ☺ ☺ ☺ ☺ ☺ ☺ ☺ ☺
Fall	☺ ☺ ☺ ☺ ☺

How many children voted in all?

25 Season
___label___

Use the bar graph to solve the problem.

2 How many fewer children like red than blue?

5 childrens
___label___

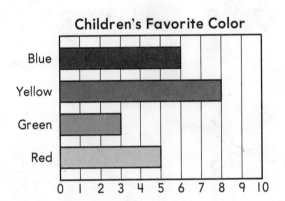

Children's Favorite Color

3 How many more children like yellow than green?

8 childrens
___label___

4 Make a bar graph to show the data in the table.

Math Awards

	Number of Awards
First Grade	5
Second Grade	9
Third Grade	7
Fourth Grade	4

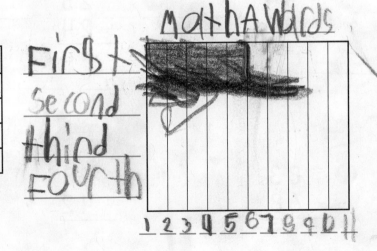

Math Awards

First
Second
third
Fourth

1 2 3 4 5 6 7 8 9 10 11

Name _____ Date _____

Add or subtract.

1 $8 - 7 =$ $\boxed{1}$ 2 $19 - 15 =$ $\boxed{4}$ 3 $7 - 6 =$ $\boxed{1}$

4 $7 + 8 =$ $\boxed{14}$ 5 $9 + 3 =$ $\boxed{12}$ 6 $10 + 10 =$ $\boxed{20}$

7
$$\begin{array}{r} 36 \\ -14 \\ \hline 22 \end{array}$$

8
$$\begin{array}{r} 60 \\ -35 \\ \hline 35 \end{array}$$

9
$$\begin{array}{r} 58 \\ -23 \\ \hline 35 \end{array}$$

10
$$\begin{array}{r} 44 \\ +20 \\ \hline 54 \end{array}$$

11
$$\begin{array}{r} 25 \\ +24 \\ \hline 49 \end{array}$$

12
$$\begin{array}{r} 17 \\ +55 \\ \hline 60 \end{array}$$

13
$$\begin{array}{r} 83 \\ -68 \\ \hline 25 \end{array}$$

14
$$\begin{array}{r} 58 \\ -42 \\ \hline 16 \end{array}$$

15
$$\begin{array}{r} 90 \\ -29 \\ \hline 79 \end{array}$$

Name _____   Date _____

Use the table.

Roses Picked	
Brad	7
Mark	9
Pam	8
Luis	5

1 Make a picture graph to show the data in the table.

Title: _____Candy Numbre_____

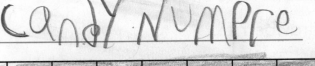

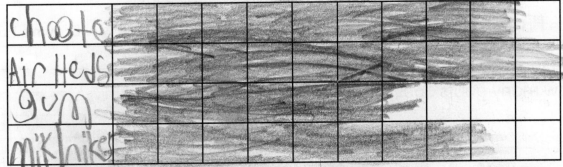

2 Make a bar graph to show the data in the table.

Title: _____Eriads Numbre_____

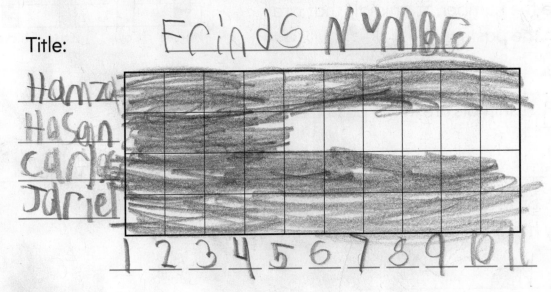

3 Use the picture graph. Choose the correct statements.

Strawberries								
Paula	🍓	🍓	🍓	🍓				
Reynaldo	🍓	🍓	🍓	🍓	🍓	🍓		

○ Paula has 2 more strawberries than Reynaldo.

◉ Reynaldo has 2 more strawberries than Paula.

◉ Paula and Reynaldo have 10 strawberries in all.

○ Reynaldo has 5 strawberries.

Use the bar graph to solve the problems.

4 The farm has 5 more goats than pigs. How many goats does the farm have?

8   goets
_____
label

5 All of the horses and cows are in the pasture. Then 5 go back to the barn. Circle the number of animals that are still in the pasture.

10

⟨11⟩   animals are in the pasture.

16

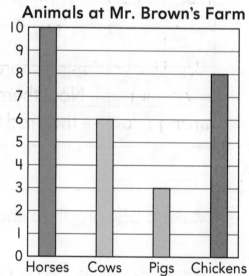

Animals at Mr. Brown's Farm

(bar graph: Horses 10, Cows 6, Pigs 3, Chickens 8)

6 If Mr. Brown's farm gets 3 more pigs, how many more horses than pigs will there be?

4   horses
_____
label

Use the bar graph.
Which statements are correct?
Choose Yes or No.

**Colors of Flowers in
Mrs. Singer's Garden**

7 There are 3 more purple flowers than
yellow flowers.

○ Yes   ○ No

8 There are 25 flowers in Mrs. Singer's
garden in all.

○ Yes   ○ No

9 If 4 of the yellow flowers are tulips and the
rest are daffodils, there must be 7 daffodils.

○ Yes   ○ No

10 Mrs. Singer plants 6 more orange flowers
in her garden. Now there are 2 more
orange flowers than red flowers.

○ Yes   ○ No

Circle the correct answer to complete the sentence.

11 At | 6:00 A.M.
         6:00 P.M. | Joel watches the sunrise.

---

12 Owen has dinner at | 7:00 A.M.
                          7:00 P.M.

---

13 Lara has lunch at | 12:00 A.M.
                          12:00 P.M.

Write the time on each digital clock.

⑭

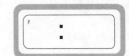

⑮

⑯

⑰ The football game starts at 1:40. Draw
hands on the clock to show the time.

Mac arrives at the football field at 1:55.
Does he see the start of the game?
Explain how you know.

_____

_____

_____

Solve. Draw comparison bars.

⑱ Elise picks 28 peaches. She picks
14 fewer than Charlie. How many
peaches does Charlie pick?

_____
| | _____
| | label

All in a Day

1 Terri, Kat, and Dana swim at 3:30. Show on
the clocks the time that they swim.

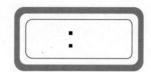

2 The table shows how many
days they swim in one
week. Make a picture graph
to show the data. Draw one
circle for each day. Then make
a bar graph to show the data.

Days Children Swim	
Terri	3
Kat	2
Dana	5

3 Write an *is greater than* statement about the data.
Write an *is less than* statement about the data.

_____

_____

_____

_____

Use the Days Children Swim graphs.
Complete each sentence.

4 Dana swims _____ more days than Terri.

5 Kat swims _____ fewer days than Dana.

6 Terri swims 1 _____ day than Kat.

7 Chad swims 4 days a week. Write a question that
compares the days Chad swims to the days another
child swims. Then solve.

_____

_____

_____

_____

Dear Family:

In this unit, children will learn how to add 3-digit numbers that have totals up to 1,000.

Children begin the unit by learning to count to 1,000. They count by ones from a number, over the hundred, and into the next hundred. For example, 498, 499, 500, 501, 502, 503. You can help your child practice counting aloud to 1,000. Listen carefully as he or she crosses over the hundred.

Children will learn to write numbers to 1,000. Some children will write 5003 instead of 503 for five hundred three. Using Secret Code Cards will help children write the numbers correctly.

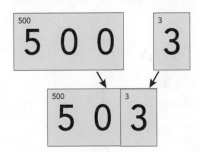

Help your child count small objects by making groups of 10 and then groups of 100. When the groups are made, help your child write the number of objects. This is a good way to help children recognize the difference between 5,003 and 503.

Please contact me if you have any questions or concerns. Thank you for helping your child learn about numbers to 1,000.

Sincerely,
Your child's teacher

CC SS Unit 6 addresses the following standards from the Common Core State Standards for Mathematics: **2.OA.A.1, 2.NBT.A.1, 2.NBT.A.1.a, 2.NBT.A.1.b, 2.NBT.A.2, 2.NBT.A.3, 2.NBT.A.4, 2.NBT.B.5, 2.NBT.B.7, 2.NBT.B.8, 2.NBT.B.9, 2.MD.C.8,** and all Mathematical Practices.

Estimada familia:

En esta unidad los niños aprenderán cómo sumar números de 3 dígitos con totales de hasta 1,000.

Los niños comienzan la unidad aprendiendo a contar hasta 1,000. Cuentan de uno en uno a partir de un número, llegan a la centena y comienzan con la siguiente centena. Por ejemplo, 498, 499, 500, 501, 502, 503. Puede ayudar a su niño a practicar, contando en voz alta hasta 1,000. Ponga atención cada vez que llegue a una nueva centena.

Los niños aprenderán a escribir los números hasta 1,000. Tal vez, algunos niños escriban 5003 en vez de 503 al intentar escribir quinientos tres. Usar las Tarjetas de código secreto los ayudará a escribir correctamente los números.

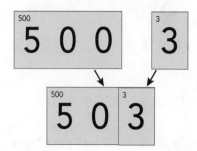

Ayude a su niño a contar objetos pequeños formando grupos de 10 y luego, grupos de 100. Cuando formen los grupos, ayúdelo a escribir el número de objetos. Esta es una buena manera de ayudar a los niños a reconocer la diferencia entre 5,003 y 503.

Si tiene alguna duda o pregunta, por favor comuníquese conmigo. Gracias por ayudar a su niño a aprender a contar hasta 1,000.

Atentamente,
El maestro de su niño

En la Unidad 6 se aplican los siguientes estándares de los Estándares estatales comunes de matemáticas: **2.OA.A.1, 2.NBT.A.1, 2.NBT.A.1.a, 2.NBT.A.1.b, 2.NBT.A.2, 2.NBT.A.3, 2.NBT.A.4, 2.NBT.B.5, 2.NBT.B.7, 2.NBT.B.8, 2.NBT.B.9, 2.MD.C.8 y todos los de** Prácticas matemáticas.

ungroup

opposite operations

Ungroup when you need more ones or tens to subtract.

$$\begin{array}{r}
1\overset{12}{}\\
0\;7\;14\\
\cancel{1}\;\cancel{3}\;\cancel{4}\\
-\;7\;8\\
\hline
5\;6
\end{array}$$

Addition and subtraction are opposite operations.

$$5 + 9 = 14$$
$$14 - 9 = 5$$

Use addition to check subtraction. Use subtraction to check addition.

Name _____

Represent 3-Digit Numbers

Write the number that is represented.

1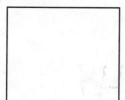

$\underline{133}$

2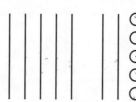

$\underline{178}$

Draw boxes, sticks, and circles to represent the number.

3 164

4 120

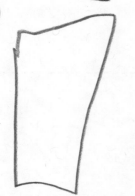

CC SS Content Standards **2.NBT.A.1, 2.NBT.A.1.a, 2.NBT.A.1.b, 2.NBT.A.2, 2.NBT.A.3**
Mathematical Practices **MP2, MP4, MP5, MP6**

Represent 3-Digit Numbers (continued)

Write the number that is represented.

⑤

244

⑥

551

Draw boxes, sticks, and circles to represent the number.

⑦ 382

✓ **Check Understanding**

Ask a friend to name a 3-digit number.
Draw boxes, sticks, and circles to represent
that number.

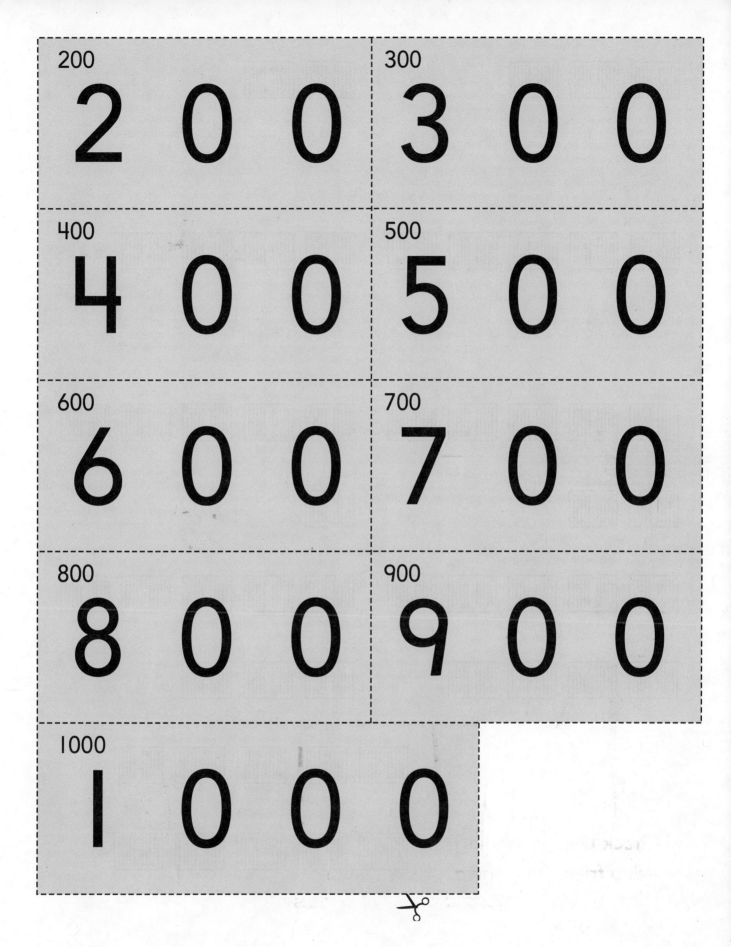

200
2 0 0

300
3 0 0

400
4 0 0

500
5 0 0

600
6 0 0

700
7 0 0

800
8 0 0

900
9 0 0

1000
1 0 0 0

Secret Code Cards (200–1000) **313**

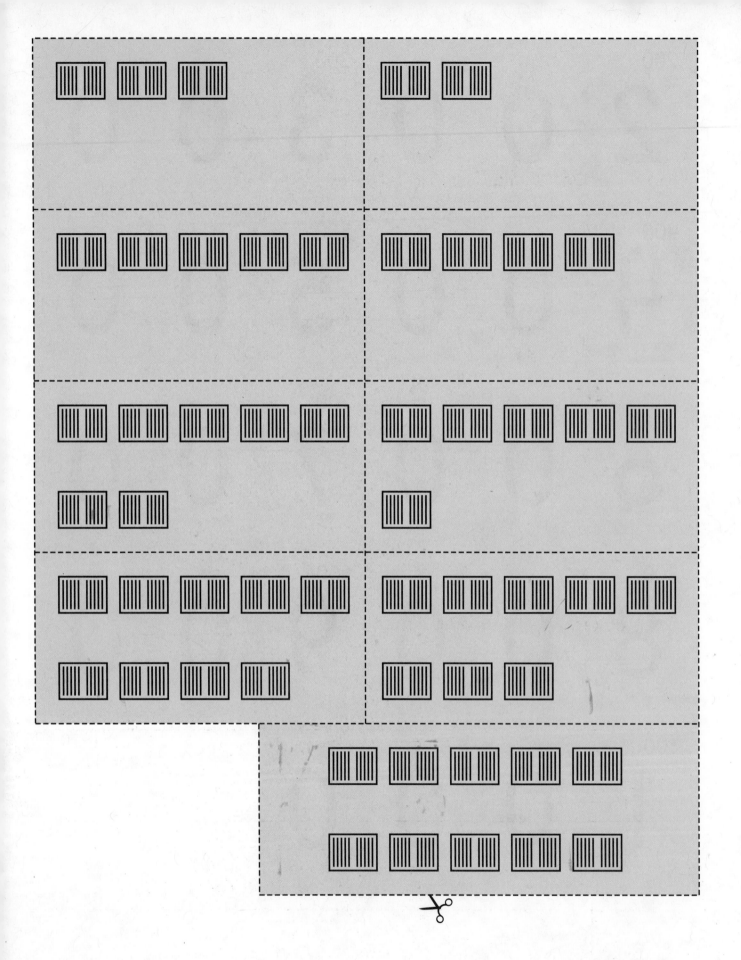

Secret Code Cards (200–1000)

Name _____

Review the Use of Boxes, Sticks, and Circles to Represent Numbers

Write the number that is shown by the drawing.

1

Hundreds	Tens	Ones
6	7	0

Total 670

2

Hundreds	Tens	Ones
3	3	5

Total 335

3

Hundreds	Tens	Ones
4	9	9

Total 499

Draw boxes, sticks, and circles to show the number.

4 740

5 876

6 294

7 502

Content Standards 2.NBT.A.1, 2.NBT.A.3
Mathematical Practices MP2, MP3, MP6

Expanded Form

Write the hundreds, tens, and ones.

⑧ 382 = 300 + 80 + 2   ⑨ 738 = 700 + 30 + 8
   H T O

⑩ 526 = 500 + 20 + 6   ⑪ 267 = 200 + 60 + 7

___

Write the number.

⑫ 400 + 50 + 9 = 459   ⑬ 800 + 10 + 3 = 813
                H T O

⑭ 100 + 70 + 5 = 175   ⑮ 600 + 40 + 1 = 641

___

Write the number that makes the equation true.

⑯ 495 = 5 + 900 + 40   ⑰ 7 + 200 = 700

⑱ 864 = 400 + 6 + 80   ⑲ 800 + 40 = 400

⑳ 700 = 70 + 300   ㉑ 60 + 500 + 3 = 653

㉒ 200 = 2 + 400   ㉓ 9 + 90 + 200 = 992

㉔ 462 = 2 + 400 + 484   ㉕ 977 + 90 + 700 = 798

㉖ 523 = 20 + 3 + 523   ㉗ 422 + 4 + 200 = 224

✔ **Check Understanding**

Describe how the Secret Code Cards can be
used to show the expanded form of a number.

    Place Value

Name _____

Solve and Discuss

Write <, >, or =.

1 635  735

2 527  527

3 820 518

4 327 372

5 975 987

6 321 567

7 267 267

8 271 172

9 654 564

10 750 507

What's the Error?

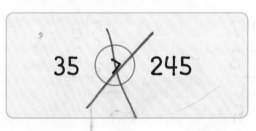

35 > 245

I know that 3 is greater than 2. Did I make a mistake?

11 Draw boxes, sticks, and circles to help Puzzled Penguin.

35 245

© Houghton Mifflin Harcourt Publishing Company

Compare Numbers

Write <, >, or =.

12 620 ⑦ 62

13 510 ⑤ 150

14 71 ⑥ 315

15 357 ⑦ 218

16 359 ⑨ 359

17 376 ⑥ 476

18 291 ⑦ 191

19 333 ⑦ 9

PATH to FLUENCY **Add or Subtract Within 100**

Add.

20 $35 + 7 =$ _42_

21 $6 + 77 =$ _83_

22 $12 + 4 =$ _16_

23
$$\begin{array}{r} 19 \\ + 60 \\ \hline 79 \end{array}$$

24
$$\begin{array}{r} 35 \\ + 42 \\ \hline 77 \end{array}$$

25
$$\begin{array}{r} 27 \\ + 73 \\ \hline 91 \end{array}$$

26
$$\begin{array}{r} 58 \\ + 4 \\ \hline 51 \end{array}$$

Subtract.

27
$$\begin{array}{r} 100 \\ - 52 \\ \hline 158 \end{array}$$

28
$$\begin{array}{r} 98 \\ - 35 \\ \hline 12 \end{array}$$

29
$$\begin{array}{r} 83 \\ - 78 \\ \hline 11 \end{array}$$

30
$$\begin{array}{r} 71 \\ - 35 \\ \hline 16 \end{array}$$

 Check Understanding

Explain how to compare 728 and 723.

Count Over a Hundred by Ones and by Tens

Count by ones. Write the numbers.

1 396 397 <u>398</u> <u>399</u> <u>400</u> <u>401</u> <u>402</u> <u>403</u> 404

2 594 595 <u>596</u> <u>597</u> <u>598</u> <u>599</u> <u>600</u> <u>601</u> 602

3 297 298 <u>299</u> <u>300</u> <u>301</u> <u>302</u> <u>303</u> <u>304</u> 305

4 495 <u>496</u> <u>497</u> <u>498</u> <u>499</u> <u>500</u> <u>501</u> <u>502</u> 503

5 598 <u>599</u> <u>600</u> <u>601</u> <u>602</u> <u>603</u> <u>604</u> <u>605</u> 606

6 697 <u>698</u> <u>699</u> <u>700</u> <u>701</u> <u>702</u> <u>703</u> <u>704</u> 705

Count by tens. Write the numbers.

7 460 470 <u>480</u> <u>490</u> <u>500</u> <u>510</u> <u>520</u> <u>530</u> 540

8 370 380 <u>390</u> <u>400</u> <u>410</u> <u>420</u> <u>430</u> <u>440</u> 450

9 640 650 <u>660</u> <u>670</u> <u>680</u> <u>690</u> <u>700</u> <u>710</u> 720

10 580 <u>590</u> <u>610</u> <u>620</u> <u>630</u> <u>640</u> <u>650</u> <u>660</u> 660

11 750 <u>760</u> <u>770</u> <u>780</u> <u>790</u> <u>800</u> <u>810</u> <u>830</u> 830

12 830 <u>840</u> <u>850</u> <u>860</u> <u>870</u> <u>880</u> <u>890</u> <u>900</u> 910

Read and Write Number Names

You can write numbers with words or symbols.

1 one	11 eleven	10 ten	100 one hundred
2 two	12 twelve	20 twenty	200 two hundred
3 three	13 thirteen	30 thirty	300 three hundred
4 four	14 fourteen	40 forty	400 four hundred
5 five	15 fifteen	50 fifty	500 five hundred
6 six	16 sixteen	60 sixty	600 six hundred
7 seven	17 seventeen	70 seventy	700 seven hundred
8 eight	18 eighteen	80 eighty	800 eight hundred
9 nine	19 nineteen	90 ninety	900 nine hundred
			1,000 one thousand

Write each number.

⑬ one hundred twenty-five _____ ⑭ four hundred fifty-eight _____

⑮ six hundred thirty-one _____ ⑯ nine hundred sixty-two _____

⑰ eight hundred forty _____ ⑱ seven hundred three _____

Write each number name.

⑲ 500 _____

⑳ 650 _____

㉑ 605 _____

㉒ 1,000 _____

 Check Understanding

Write a 3-digit number. Trade with a friend. Write the number name for your friend's 3-digit number.

Count by Ones and by Tens

Name _____

Add Numbers with 1, 2, and 3 Digits

Solve.

1. $200 + 200 =$ _____ $200 + 20 =$ _____ $200 + 2 =$ _____

   $300 + 300 =$ _____ $300 + 30 =$ _____ $300 + 3 =$ _____

   $400 + 400 =$ _____ $400 + 40 =$ _____ $400 + 4 =$ _____

   $500 + 500 =$ _____ $500 + 50 =$ _____ $500 + 5 =$ _____

2. $600 + 200 =$ _____ $20 + 600 =$ _____ $2 + 600 =$ _____

   $700 + 300 =$ _____ $30 + 700 =$ _____ $3 + 700 =$ _____

   $800 + 100 =$ _____ $10 + 800 =$ _____ $1 + 800 =$ _____

   $900 + 100 =$ _____ $10 + 900 =$ _____ $1 + 900 =$ _____

   $100 + 900 =$ _____ $90 + 100 =$ _____ $9 + 100 =$ _____

3. $100 + 134 =$ _____ $100 + 34 =$ _____ $4 + 100 =$ _____

   $200 + 245 =$ _____ $200 + 45 =$ _____ $200 + 5 =$ _____

   $300 + 356 =$ _____ $56 + 300 =$ _____ $6 + 300 =$ _____

   $400 + 467 =$ _____ $400 + 67 =$ _____ $400 + 7 =$ _____

   $500 + 478 =$ _____ $78 + 500 =$ _____ $8 + 500 =$ _____

Solve and Discuss

Solve each word problem. Use Secret Code Cards
or make proof drawings if you wish.

④ A camping club buys some
raisins. They buy 3 cartons that
have 100 bags each. They also
have 24 bags left from their last
trip. How many bags of raisins
does the club have?

［　　　］ ＿＿＿＿＿＿＿＿＿＿
　　　　　　label

⑤ Two friends want to make
necklaces. They buy 1 package
of one hundred red beads,
1 package of one hundred blue
beads, and 1 package of one
hundred green beads. They
already have 12 loose beads.
How many beads do they have
altogether?

［　　　］ ＿＿＿＿＿＿＿＿＿＿
　　　　　　label

⑥ All of the students at a school
go out on the playground.
They form 6 groups of one
hundred students and 5 groups
of ten students. There are
8 students left. How many
students go to the school?

［　　　］ ＿＿＿＿＿＿＿＿＿＿
　　　　　　label

 Check Understanding

Solve.

4 +
two hundred +
3 groups of ten = ［　　　］

　　　　　　Add Ones, Tens, and Hundreds

Count the hundreds, tens, and ones.
Then write the total.

①

_____ _____ _____   Total _____
Hundreds   Tens   Ones

Write the hundreds, tens, and ones.
Then write the number name.

② 749 = _____ + _____ + _____   _____

Write <, >, or =.

③ 641 ◯ 614

Count by 10s. Write the numbers.

④ 370 380 _____ _____ _____ _____ _____ _____ 450

Solve.   Show your work.

⑤ Victor bought some stickers. He bought
3 pages that had 100 stickers on each
page. He also bought 27 extra stickers.
How many stickers did he buy in all?

            label

Name _____

Date _____

Add or subtract.

1 $19 - 6 =$ ☐

2 $12 - 3 =$ ☐

3 $7 - 2 =$ ☐

4 $10 + 10 =$ ☐

5 $14 + 3 =$ ☐

6 $8 + 2 =$ ☐

7
$$\begin{array}{r} 31 \\ -\ 20 \\ \hline \end{array}$$

8
$$\begin{array}{r} 58 \\ -\ 49 \\ \hline \end{array}$$

9
$$\begin{array}{r} 36 \\ -\ 2 \\ \hline \end{array}$$

10
$$\begin{array}{r} 54 \\ +\ 37 \\ \hline \end{array}$$

11
$$\begin{array}{r} 15 \\ +\ 34 \\ \hline \end{array}$$

12
$$\begin{array}{r} 29 \\ +\ 57 \\ \hline \end{array}$$

13
$$\begin{array}{r} 86 \\ -\ 58 \\ \hline \end{array}$$

14
$$\begin{array}{r} 100 \\ -\ 47 \\ \hline \end{array}$$

15
$$\begin{array}{r} 95 \\ -\ 39 \\ \hline \end{array}$$

Dear Family:

Your child is now learning how to add 3-digit numbers. The methods children use are similar to those used for adding 2-digit numbers.

New Groups Below

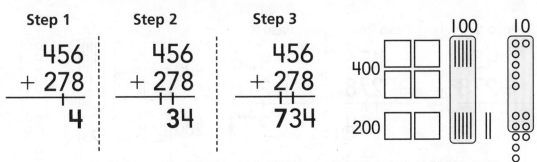

Children put the new 1 hundred or 1 ten on the line instead of at the top of the column. Many children find this less confusing because:

- They can see the 14.
- It is easier to add the 1 after they add the 5 and the 7.

Show All Totals

$$456$$
$$+ 278$$

hundreds → 600
tens → 120
ones → 14
734

Children see the hundreds, tens, and ones they are adding. These can also be seen when they make a math drawing like the one above.

Children may use any method that they understand, can explain, and can do fairly quickly. They should use hundreds, tens, and ones language to explain. This shows that they understand that they are adding 4 hundreds and 2 hundreds, not 4 and 2.

Please contact me if you have questions or comments.

Sincerely,
Your child's teacher

CC SS Unit 6 addresses the following standards from the Common Core State Standards for Mathematics: 2.OA.A.1, 2.NBT.A.1, 2.NBT.A.1.a, 2.NBT.A.1.b, 2.NBT.A.2, 2.NBT.A.3, 2.NBT.A.4, 2.NBT.B.5, 2.NBT.B.7, 2.NBT.B.8, 2.NBT.B.9, 2.MD.C.8, and all Mathematical Practices.

Estimada familia:

Ahora su niño está aprendiendo a sumar números de 3 dígitos. Los métodos que los niños usarán son semejantes a los usados para sumar numeros de 2 dígitos.

Grupos nuevos abajo

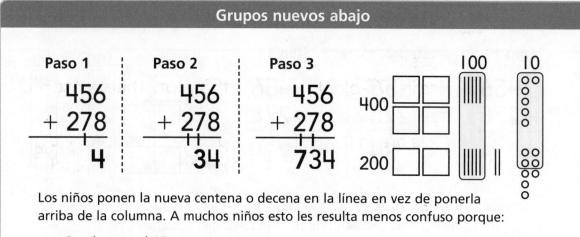

Los niños ponen la nueva centena o decena en la línea en vez de ponerla arriba de la columna. A muchos niños esto les resulta menos confuso porque:

- Pueden ver el 14.
- Es más fácil sumar el 1 después de que sumaron 5 y 7.

Mostrar todos los totales

$$456$$
$$+\ 278$$

centenas ⟶ 600
decenas ⟶ 120
unidades ⟶ 14
$$\overline{734}$$

Los niños ven las centenas, las decenas y las unidades que están sumando. Esto también se puede observar cuando hacen un dibujo matemático como el de arriba.

Los niños pueden usar cualquier método que comprendan, puedan explicar y puedan hacer relativamente rápido. Para explicar deben usar un lenguaje relacionado con centenas, decenas y unidades. Esto demuestra que entienden que están sumando 4 centenas y 2 centenas, no 4 y 2.

Si tiene alguna duda o pregunta, por favor comuníquese conmigo.

Atentamente,
El maestro de su niño

© Houghton Mifflin Harcourt Publishing Company

En la Unidad 6 se aplican los siguientes estándares de los Estándares estatales comunes de matemáticas: **2.OA.A.1, 2.NBT.A.1, 2.NBT.A.1.a, 2.NBT.A.1.b, 2.NBT.A.2, 2.NBT.A.3, 2.NBT.A.4, 2.NBT.B.5, 2.NBT.B.7, 2.NBT.B.8, 2.NBT.B.9, 2.MD.C.8** y todos los de Prácticas matemáticas.

Name _____

Solve and Discuss

Solve each word problem.
Be ready to explain what you did.

1 Mrs. Ruth makes a display of plant and fish fossils for the library. She puts in 478 plant fossils. She puts in 67 fish fossils. How many fossils are in the display?

[ ] _____
label

2 The members of the nature club planted pine and birch trees this year. There were 496 birch trees planted and 283 pine trees planted. How many pine and birch trees were planted in all?

[ ] _____
label

3 There are 818 ducks entered in the Rubber Duck River Race. Then 182 more are added. How many ducks are in the race now?

[ ] _____
label

4 There are 189 children at Camp Sunshine. There are 375 children at Camp Bluebird. How many children are there at the two camps?

[ ] _____
label

Practice 3-Digit Addition

Add using any method. Make a proof drawing if it helps.

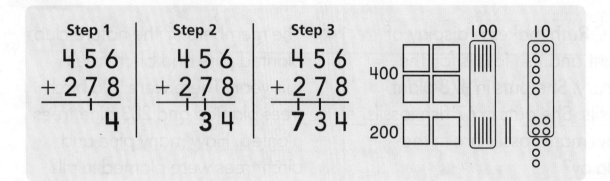

Step 1	Step 2	Step 3
456	456	456
+278	+278	+278
4	34	734

(5)
```
  375
+ 482
```

(6)
```
  148
+ 236
```

(7)
```
  584
+  61
```

(8)
```
  168
+ 674
```

(9)
```
   89
+ 376
```

(10)
```
  563
+ 157
```

(11)
```
  497
+ 259
```

(12)
```
  124
+ 563
```

(13)
```
  348
+ 239
```

✓ **Check Understanding**

Draw a proof diagram for Exercise 11.

3-Digit Addition

Name _____

New Ten or New Hundred

Add. Use any method. Make a proof drawing if it helps.

1
$$\begin{array}{r} 2\ 3\ 6 \\ +\ 4\ 7\ 8 \\ \hline \end{array}$$

Make a new ten? _____

Make a new hundred? _____

2 $183 + 517 =$ _____

Make a new ten? _____

Make a new hundred? _____

3 $93 + 485 =$ _____

Make a new ten? _____

Make a new hundred? _____

4
$$\begin{array}{r} 3\ 6\ 8 \\ +\ 2\ 5\ 7 \\ \hline \end{array}$$

Make a new ten? _____

Make a new hundred? _____

5 $347 + 37 =$ _____

Make a new ten? _____

Make a new hundred? _____

6 $645 + 87 =$ _____

Make a new ten? _____

Make a new hundred? _____

CC SS Content Standards 2.NBT.B.7, 2.NBT.B.9
Mathematical Practices MP3, MP5, MP6, MP8

Discuss 3-Digit Addition **329**

New Ten, New Hundred, or New Thousand

Add. Use any method. Draw a proof drawing if it helps.

7
```
  1 9 5
+ 1 7 2
```

Make a new ten? _____

Make a new hundred? _____

Make a new thousand? _____

8
```
  3 0 0
+ 7 0 0
```

Make a new ten? _____

Make a new hundred? _____

Make a new thousand? _____

9 360 + 640 = _____

Make a new ten? _____

Make a new hundred? _____

Make a new thousand? _____

10 75 + 823 = _____

Make a new ten? _____

Make a new hundred? _____

Make a new thousand? _____

11 905 + 95 = _____

Make a new ten? _____

Make a new hundred? _____

Make a new thousand? _____

12 413 + 587 = _____

Make a new ten? _____

Make a new hundred? _____

Make a new thousand? _____

 Check Understanding

Explain how you found the sum for Exercise 9.

Discuss 3-Digit Addition

Find the Hidden Animal

Directions for the puzzle on page 332:

1 Find one of the sums below. Then look for that sum in the puzzle grid. Color in that puzzle piece.

2 Find all 20 sums. Color the puzzle pieces with the sums. Color in all 20 correct answers.

3 Name the hidden animal. It is a(n) _____.

$$
\begin{array}{r} 524 \\ + 247 \\ \hline \end{array}
\qquad
\begin{array}{r} 287 \\ + 164 \\ \hline \end{array}
\qquad
\begin{array}{r} 384 \\ + 375 \\ \hline \end{array}
\qquad
\begin{array}{r} 456 \\ + 174 \\ \hline \end{array}
\qquad
\begin{array}{r} 327 \\ + 265 \\ \hline \end{array}
$$

$$
\begin{array}{r} 207 \\ + 595 \\ \hline \end{array}
\qquad
\begin{array}{r} 248 \\ + 376 \\ \hline \end{array}
\qquad
\begin{array}{r} 282 \\ + 457 \\ \hline \end{array}
\qquad
\begin{array}{r} 548 \\ + 387 \\ \hline \end{array}
\qquad
\begin{array}{r} 233 \\ + 288 \\ \hline \end{array}
$$

$$
\begin{array}{r} 367 \\ + 265 \\ \hline \end{array}
\qquad
\begin{array}{r} 293 \\ + 595 \\ \hline \end{array}
\qquad
\begin{array}{r} 284 \\ + 376 \\ \hline \end{array}
\qquad
\begin{array}{r} 537 \\ + 463 \\ \hline \end{array}
\qquad
\begin{array}{r} 138 \\ + 327 \\ \hline \end{array}
$$

$$
\begin{array}{r} 286 \\ + 78 \\ \hline \end{array}
\qquad
\begin{array}{r} 407 \\ + 266 \\ \hline \end{array}
\qquad
\begin{array}{r} 503 \\ + 148 \\ \hline \end{array}
\qquad
\begin{array}{r} 78 \\ + 65 \\ \hline \end{array}
\qquad
\begin{array}{r} 192 \\ + 339 \\ \hline \end{array}
$$

See page 331 for directions on how to solve the puzzle.

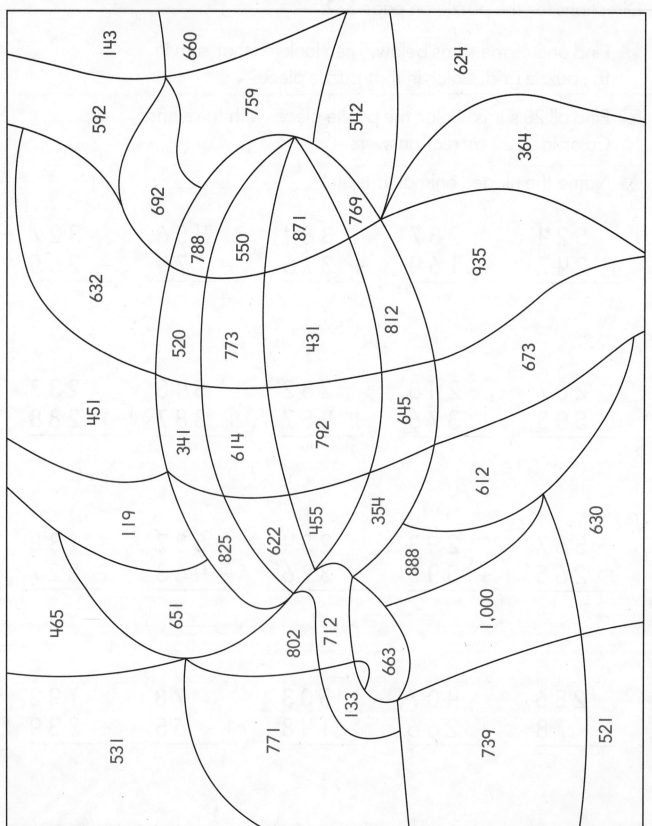

Discuss 3-Digit Addition

Name _____

Adding Up to Solve Word Problems

Solve each word problem.

Show your work.

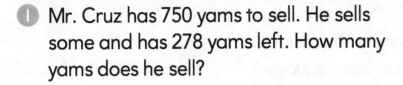

① Mr. Cruz has 750 yams to sell. He sells some and has 278 yams left. How many yams does he sell?

[   ] _____
         label

② At the end of February there are 692 houses in our town. Some new houses are built in March. At the end of March there are 976 houses. How many houses are built in March?

[   ] _____
         label

③ Delia has 224 shells in her collection. She gives some to her sister. Now she has 162 shells. How many shells did she give away?

[   ] _____
         label

④ On Saturday, 703 people go to a movie. 194 go in the afternoon. The rest go in the evening. How many people go to the movie in the evening?

[   ] _____
         label

Adding Up to Solve Word Problems (continued)

Solve.   **Show your work.**

5 Jeremy makes 525 coasters that are circles
or squares as gifts for his family. 347 coasters
are circles. How many coasters are squares?

[ ] _____
                label

(PATH to FLUENCY) Add and Subtract Within 100

Add.

6　3 2
　　+ 5 0

7　4 2
　　+ 5 7

8　5 7
　　+ 4 3

9　4 4
　　+ 　7

Subtract.

10　9 8
　　− 2 4

11　1 0 0
　　−　 3 1

12　4 3
　　− 3 8

13　6 1
　　− 2 9

✓ Check Understanding

Use the Adding Up Method to solve.

$251 + \boxed{} = 632$

$251 + \underline{} = 260$

$260 + \underline{} = 300$

$300 + \underline{} = 600$

$600 + \underline{} = 632$

$251 + \boxed{} = 632$

Word Problems: Unknown Addends

Add.

1.   3 1 8
    + 2 5 3

2.   4 8 6
    + 3 5 7

Solve.   **Show your work.**

3. Mrs. Green drives 357 miles on Monday and 292 miles on Tuesday. How many miles does she drive in all?

☐☐☐ _____
      label

4. Mrs. Brach made 400 quilts to sell. After she sold some, she had 174 left. How many quilts did she sell?

☐☐☐ _____
      label

5. On Friday, 834 meals were served. 458 meals were served at breakfast. The rest were served at lunch. How many meals were served at lunch?

☐☐☐ _____
      label

Name _____ **Date** _____

Add or subtract.

1 $15 - 8 =$ ☐

2 $16 - 13 =$ ☐

3 $14 - 4 =$ ☐

4 $8 + 9 =$ ☐

5 $11 + 6 =$ ☐

6 $9 + 11 =$ ☐

7
$$\begin{array}{r} 26 \\ -\ 5 \\ \hline \end{array}$$

8
$$\begin{array}{r} 56 \\ +42 \\ \hline \end{array}$$

9
$$\begin{array}{r} 26 \\ -13 \\ \hline \end{array}$$

10
$$\begin{array}{r} 70 \\ -63 \\ \hline \end{array}$$

11
$$\begin{array}{r} 30 \\ +48 \\ \hline \end{array}$$

12
$$\begin{array}{r} 29 \\ +25 \\ \hline \end{array}$$

13
$$\begin{array}{r} 57 \\ +43 \\ \hline \end{array}$$

14
$$\begin{array}{r} 23 \\ +68 \\ \hline \end{array}$$

15
$$\begin{array}{r} 38 \\ +37 \\ \hline \end{array}$$

Dear Family:

Your child is now learning how to subtract 3-digit numbers. The most important part is understanding and being able to explain a method. Children may use any method that they understand, can explain, and can perform fairly quickly.

Expanded Method

Step 1   **Step 2**

$$\begin{aligned} 432 &= 400 + 30 + 2 = \overset{300}{\cancel{400}} + \overset{\overset{120}{20}}{\cancel{30}} + \overset{12}{\cancel{2}} \\ -273 &= 200 + 70 + 3 = 200 + 70 + 3 \end{aligned}$$

Step 3 $\left\{ \begin{aligned} &100 + 50 + 9 \\ &= 159 \end{aligned} \right.$

Step 1 "Expand" each number to show that it is made up of hundreds, tens, and ones.

Step 2 Check to see if there are enough ones to subtract from. If not, ungroup a ten into 10 ones and add it to the existing ones. Check to see if there are enough tens to subtract from. If not, ungroup a hundred into 10 tens and add it to the existing tens. Children may also ungroup from the left.

Step 3 Subtract to find the answer. Children may subtract from left to right or right to left.

Ungroup First Method

Step 1 Check to see if there are enough ones and tens to subtract from. Ungroup where needed.

Look inside 432. Ungroup 432 and rename it as 3 hundreds, 12 tens, and 12 ones.

Ungroup from the left:

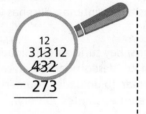

Ungroup from the right:

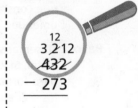

Step 2 Subtract to find the answer. Children may subtract from the left or from the right.

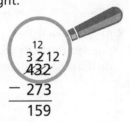

In explaining any method they use, children are expected to use "hundreds, tens, and ones" language and drawings to show that they understand place value.

Please contact me if you have questions or comments.

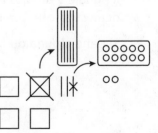

Sincerely,
Your child's teacher

© Houghton Mifflin Harcourt Publishing Company

Estimada familia:

Su niño está aprendiendo a restar números de 3 dígitos. Lo más importante es comprender y saber explicar un método. Los niños pueden usar cualquier método que comprendan, puedan explicar y puedan hacer relativamente rápido.

Método extendido

Paso 1   Paso 2

$$432 = 400 + 30 + 2 = 400 + 30 + 2$$
$$- 273 = 200 + 70 + 3 = 200 + 70 + 3$$

Paso 3 $\begin{cases} 100 + 50 + 9 \\ = 159 \end{cases}$

Paso 1 "Extender" cada número para mostrar que consta de centenas, decenas y unidades.

Paso 2 Observar si hay suficientes unidades para restar. Si no, desagrupar una decena para formar 10 unidades y sumarlas a las unidades existentes. Observar si hay suficientes decenas para restar. Si no, desagrupar una centena para formar 10 decenas y sumarlas a las decenas existentes. Los niños también pueden desagrupar por la izquierda.

Paso 3 Restar para hallar la respuesta. Los niños pueden restar de izquierda a derecha o de derecha a izquierda.

Método de desagrupar primero

Paso 1 Observar si hay suficientes unidades y decenas para restar. Desagrupar cuando haga falta.

Mirar dentro de 432. Desagrupar 432 y volver a nombrarlo como 3 centenas, 12 decenas y 12 unidades.

Desagrupar   Desagrupar
por la izquierda: por la derecha:

Paso 2 Restar para hallar la respuesta. Los niños pueden restar empezando por la izquierda o por la derecha.

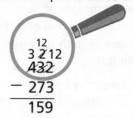

Para explicar cualquier método que usen, los niños deben usar lenguaje y dibujos relacionados con centenas, decenas y unidades para demostrar que comprenden el valor posicional.

Si tiene alguna duda o comentario, por favor comuníquese conmigo.

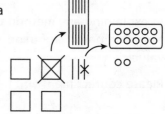

Atentamente,
El maestro de su niño

En la Unidad 6 se aplican los siguientes estándares de los Estándares estatales comunes de matemáticas: **2.OA.A.1, 2.NBT.A.1, 2.NBT.A.1.a, 2.NBT.A.1.b, 2.NBT.A.2, 2.NBT.A.3, 2.NBT.A.4, 2.NBT.B.5, 2.NBT.B.7, 2.NBT.B.8, 2.NBT.B.9, 2.MD.C.8 y todos los de** Prácticas matemáticas.

Name _____

Discuss Subtraction Problems

Solve each word problem. Use any method.
Make a proof drawing.

1 A teacher buys 200 erasers for his students. He gives 152 of them away. How many erasers does he have left over?

_____
label

2 The school cafeteria has 500 apples. Some of them are served with lunch. After lunch, there are 239 apples left. How many apples does the cafeteria serve?

_____
label

3 At the Music Megastore, there are 600 guitars for sale at the beginning of the month. At the end of the month, there are 359 guitars. How many guitars are sold?

_____
label

4 Jorge is on a basketball team. He scores 181 points one year. He scores some points in a second year, too. He scores a total of 400 points over the two years. How many points does he score the second year?

_____
label

Practice Subtracting from 1,000

Subtract. Use any method.

5
```
  1,000
–   772
```

6
```
  1,000
–   526
```

7
```
  1,000
–   843
```

8
```
  1,000
–   293
```

9
```
  1,000
–    95
```

10
```
  1,000
–   157
```

11 Elliot has 1,000 pennies. He puts 350 pennies in penny rolls. How many pennies are left?

_____ _____
label

12 Marta's class plans to collect 1,000 cans this year. They have 452 cans so far. How many more cans do they plan to collect?

_____ _____
label

 Check Understanding

Draw quick pictures to show how you solved Exercise 6.

© Houghton Mifflin Harcourt Publishing Company

Subtract from Hundreds Numbers

Name _____

VOCABULARY
ungroup

Do I Need to Ungroup?

Decide if you need to **ungroup**. If you need to ungroup, draw a magnifying glass around the top number. Then find the answer.

1
```
  5 0 8
− 3 4 6
```

Ungroup to get 10 ones? _____

Ungroup to get 10 tens? _____

2
```
  5 0 0
− 3 0 6
```

Ungroup to get 10 ones? _____

Ungroup to get 10 tens? _____

3
```
  6 7 0
− 3 4 0
```

Ungroup to get 10 ones? _____

Ungroup to get 10 tens? _____

4
```
  5 7 0
− 3 9 0
```

Ungroup to get 10 ones? _____

Ungroup to get 10 tens? _____

© Houghton Mifflin Harcourt Publishing Company

Subtract from 3-Digit Numbers with Zeros

Subtract.

⑤
```
  406
- 181
```

⑥
```
  790
- 272
```

⑦
```
  340
- 118
```

⑧
```
  507
- 438
```

⑨
```
  400
- 263
```

⑩
```
  500
- 234
```

PATH to FLUENCY Add and Subtract Within 100

Add.

⑪
```
  38
+ 44
```

⑫
```
  61
+ 17
```

⑬
```
  36
+ 64
```

⑭
```
  78
+ 19
```

Subtract.

⑮
```
  100
-  57
```

⑯
```
  92
- 40
```

⑰
```
  64
- 25
```

⑱
```
  81
- 19
```

Check Understanding

Explain how you know when to ungroup in subtraction.

Subtract from Numbers with Zeros

Name _____

Practice and Represent 3-Digit Subtraction

Solve. Show your work.

1) $\begin{array}{r} 473 \\ -354 \\ \hline \end{array}$

2) $\begin{array}{r} 828 \\ -381 \\ \hline \end{array}$

3) $\begin{array}{r} 215 \\ -161 \\ \hline \end{array}$

4) $\begin{array}{r} 526 \\ -259 \\ \hline \end{array}$

5) $\begin{array}{r} 686 \\ -259 \\ \hline \end{array}$

6) $\begin{array}{r} 917 \\ -261 \\ \hline \end{array}$

Practice and Represent 3-Digit Subtraction (continued)

Solve. Show your work.

7
```
  3 6 8
− 1 7 9
```

8
```
  9 9 9
− 2 3 6
```

What's the Error?

```
  9 0 3
−  6 4 7
───────
  3 4 4
```

Am I correct?

9 Show Puzzled Penguin how you would solve the problem.

```
  9 0 3
−  6 4 7
───────
  2 5 6
```

 Check Understanding

Explain how to ungroup to solve 752 − 384.

Subtract from Any 3-Digit Number

Name _____

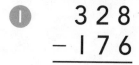

Practice with Ungrouping

Solve. Show your work.

1
```
  3 2 8
- 1 7 6
```

How many times
did you ungroup?

_____

2
```
  6 3 5
- 1 7 6
```

How many times
did you ungroup?

_____

3
```
  4 8 0
- 1 7 6
```

How many times
did you ungroup?

_____

4
```
  2 9 7
- 1 7 6
```

How many times
did you ungroup?

_____

CC SS Content Standards **2.NBT.A.1, 2.NBT.B.7, 2.NBT.B.9**
Mathematical Practices **MP1, MP2, MP6, MP7, MP8**

Practice with Ungrouping (continued)

Solve. Show your work.

5
```
  986
- 176
```

How many times
did you ungroup?

_____

6
```
  509
- 176
```

How many times
did you ungroup?

_____

7
```
  800
- 176
```

How many times
did you ungroup?

_____

8
```
  570
- 176
```

How many times
did you ungroup?

_____

✔ **Check Understanding**

Write a subtraction problem that requires
ungrouping only once.

Practice Ungrouping

Name ________________________ Date ____________

Subtract.

1. $\begin{array}{r} 508 \\ -\ 371 \\ \hline \end{array}$

2. $\begin{array}{r} 300 \\ -\ 183 \\ \hline \end{array}$

Solve.

Show your work.

3. Mr. Decker bought 300 pencils. He gave 183 of the pencils away. How many pencils does he have left over?

☐ ____________ label

4. Gina wants to save 1,000 dimes. She has saved 681 so far. How many more dimes does she need to save?

☐ ____________ label

5. Rick has 742 stamps. He gives 671 of them to Amy. How many stamps does Rick have left?

☐ ____________ label

Name _____   **Date** _____

Add or subtract.

1 $15 - 2 = \boxed{}$ **2** $19 - 6 = \boxed{}$ **3** $16 - 10 = \boxed{}$

4 $12 + 7 = \boxed{}$ **5** $9 + 5 = \boxed{}$ **6** $13 + 7 = \boxed{}$

7
$$\begin{array}{r} 38 \\ -\ 20 \\ \hline \end{array}$$

8
$$\begin{array}{r} 47 \\ -\ 43 \\ \hline \end{array}$$

9
$$\begin{array}{r} 27 \\ -\ 14 \\ \hline \end{array}$$

10
$$\begin{array}{r} 61 \\ -\ 12 \\ \hline \end{array}$$

11
$$\begin{array}{r} 35 \\ +\ 33 \\ \hline \end{array}$$

12
$$\begin{array}{r} 71 \\ +\ 19 \\ \hline \end{array}$$

13
$$\begin{array}{r} 67 \\ +\ 15 \\ \hline \end{array}$$

14
$$\begin{array}{r} 29 \\ +\ 62 \\ \hline \end{array}$$

15
$$\begin{array}{r} 69 \\ +\ 24 \\ \hline \end{array}$$

Name _____

Review Addition and Subtraction

Loop *add* or *subtract*. Check if you need to ungroup or make a new ten or hundred. Then find the answer.

①
```
  762
- 395
```

subtract

☐ ungroup to get 10 ones

☐ ungroup to get 10 tens

add

☐ make 1 new ten

☐ make 1 new hundred

②
```
  395
+ 367
```

subtract

☐ ungroup to get 10 ones

☐ ungroup to get 10 tens

add

☐ make 1 new ten

☐ make 1 new hundred

③
```
  287
- 193
```

subtract

☐ ungroup to get 10 ones

☐ ungroup to get 10 tens

add

☐ make 1 new ten

☐ make 1 new hundred

④
```
  437
+ 324
```

subtract

☐ ungroup to get 10 ones

☐ ungroup to get 10 tens

add

☐ make 1 new ten

☐ make 1 new hundred

Relate Addition and Subtraction

Decide whether you need to add or subtract.
Draw a Math Mountain. Check your answer by using
the **opposite operation**.

5.
$$\begin{array}{r} 5\ 3\ 2 \\ -\ 1\ 8\ 1 \end{array}$$ ✓

6.
$$\begin{array}{r} 5\ 3\ 2 \\ +\ 1\ 8\ 1 \end{array}$$ ✓

7.
$$\begin{array}{r} 5\ 2\ 8 \\ +\ 3\ 5\ 7 \end{array}$$ ✓

8.
$$\begin{array}{r} 1{,}0\ 0\ 0 \\ -\ \ \ 4\ 3\ 8 \end{array}$$ ✓

9.
$$\begin{array}{r} 5\ 7\ 1 \\ +\ 2\ 8\ 7 \end{array}$$ ✓

10.
$$\begin{array}{r} 9\ 0\ 4 \\ -\ 4\ 5\ 8 \end{array}$$ ✓

 Check Understanding

Draw a Math Mountain to show the solution
for 847 − 266.

     Relationships Between Addition and Subtraction Methods

Name _____

Solve and Discuss

Make a drawing. Write an equation.
Solve the problem.

1 Lucero spills a bag of marbles. 219 fall on the floor. 316 are still in the bag. How many were in the bag in the beginning?

```
┌──────┐
│      │ _____
└──────┘          label
```

2 Al counts bugs in the park. He counts 561 in March. He counts 273 fewer than that in April. How many bugs does he count in April?

```
┌──────┐
│      │ _____
└──────┘          label
```

3 Happy the Clown gives out balloons. She gives out 285 at the zoo and then gives out some more at the amusement park. Altogether she gives out 503 balloons. How many balloons does she give out at the amusement park?

```
┌──────┐
│      │ _____
└──────┘          label
```

4 Charlie the Clown gives out 842 balloons at the fun fair. He gives out 194 at the store. He gives out 367 at the playground. How many more balloons does he give out at the fun fair than at the playground?

```
┌──────┐
│      │ _____
└──────┘          label
```

Solve and Discuss (continued)

Make a drawing. Write an equation.
Solve the problem.

5 Damon collects stamps. He has 383 stamps. Then he buys 126 more at a yard sale. How many stamps does he have now?

[ ] _____
label

6 Mr. Lewis sells 438 melons. Now he has 294 melons left. How many melons did he have at the start?

[ ] _____
label

7 Ali is giving out ribbons for a race. She gave out 57 ribbons so far, and she has 349 ribbons left. How many ribbons did she have at the start?

[ ] _____
label

8 Cora collected 542 sports cards last year. She collected 247 fewer than that this year. How many cards did she collect in both years together?

[ ] _____
label

Mixed Addition and Subtraction Word Problems

Name _____

Solve and Discuss (continued)

Make a drawing. Write an equation. Solve the problem.

9 Ms. Andy is working on a puzzle. She has placed 643 pieces. There are 1,000 pieces in the puzzle. How many more pieces does she have to place?

```
┌──────────┐
│          │   _____
└──────────┘        label
```

10 In March the Shaws plant some flowers. In April they plant 178 more flowers. In the two months they plant a total of 510 flowers. How many flowers do they plant in March?

```
┌──────────┐
│          │   _____
└──────────┘        label
```

11 Jeremy has 48 action figures. Jeremy has 14 more action figures than Keith. How many action figures does Keith have?

```
┌──────────┐
│          │   _____
└──────────┘        label
```

12 Mr. Pawel gives out flyers about a play. He gives out 194 flyers at the bakery. He gives out 358 flyers at the grocery store. How many fewer flyers does he give out at the bakery than at the grocery store?

```
┌──────────┐
│          │   _____
└──────────┘        label
```

Solve and Discuss (continued)

Make a drawing. Write an equation. Solve the problem.

13 There are 675 plastic cups and 300 paper plates in a cabinet. Jaime puts more cups and plates in the cabinet. Now there are 850 cups. How many cups does Jaime add?

[ ] _____
label

14 Last week Miss Bee sold some tickets to a play. She sells 345 more this week. Altogether she sells 500 tickets. How many tickets did she sell last week?

[ ] _____
label

15 April has 98 fewer pennies than Julie has. April has 521 pennies. How many pennies does Julie have?

[ ] _____
label

 Check Understanding

Complete the comparison bars for this problem:

Ms. Vaughn has 342 buttons. She has 163 more buttons than Mr. Wheel. How many buttons does Mr. Wheel have?

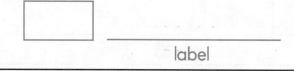

Mixed Addition and Subtraction Word Problems

Name _____

Solve Problems at the Art Fair

Many artists sell their work at art fairs.

Solve.

① On one weekend, 489 people come to the art fair on Saturday and 511 people come to the fair on Sunday. How many people come to the fair in all?

☐ _____
label

② Wendy uses silver and blue beads to make necklaces to sell. She uses 72 blue beads. She uses 38 more blue beads than silver beads. How many silver beads does she use?

☐ _____
label

③ LeBron uses tiny seed beads to make bracelets. He buys a package of seed beads with 350 red beads and 250 white beads. After he makes the bracelets for the fair, he has just 6 beads left. How many beads does he use?

☐ _____
label

Caricatures

A caricature is a drawing of a person.
The drawing looks like a cartoon.

> • Last week, an artist drew
>   146 children and 84 adults.
>
> • This week, the artist drew
>   167 children and 55 adults.

Solve. Use the information in the box above.

4 How many people did the artist draw last week?

☐ _____
       label

5 How many people did the artist draw this week?

☐ _____
       label

6 How many fewer people did the artist draw
this week than last week?

☐ _____
       label

7 Did the artist draw more children or more adults?

more _____

Focus on Mathematical Practices

Add. Subtract to check.

①   4 3 1
    + 2 7 2
_____

Subtract. Add to check.

②   5 4 3
    − 1 9 2
_____

Solve.   Show your work.

③ Jim grows 398 pounds of corn. Roberto
grows 475 pounds of corn. How many
more pounds of corn does Roberto grow
than Jim?

```
┌──────┐
│      │  _____
└──────┘       label
```

④ Joe loads 268 bales of hay onto the truck.
317 bales of hay still need to be loaded.
How many bales of hay are there altogether?

```
┌──────┐
│      │  _____
└──────┘       label
```

⑤ Lindsey lives 593 miles from May's house and
417 miles from Chad's house. How many more
miles does she live from May's house than
Chad's house?

```
┌──────┐
│      │  _____
└──────┘       label
```

Name _____

Date _____

Add or subtract.

1 $13 + 5 = \boxed{18}$

2 $19 + 1 = \boxed{20}$

3 $11 + 2 = \boxed{13}$

4 $15 - 7 = \boxed{8}$

5 $16 - 9 = \boxed{7}$

6 $14 - 12 = \boxed{2}$

7
$$\begin{array}{r} 36 \\ -26 \\ \hline 10 \end{array}$$

8
$$\begin{array}{r} 77 \\ -58 \\ \hline 21 \end{array}$$

9
$$\begin{array}{r} 31 \\ +13 \\ \hline 44 \end{array}$$

10
$$\begin{array}{r} 65 \\ +16 \\ \hline 81 \end{array}$$

11
$$\begin{array}{r} 24 \\ + 6 \\ \hline 30 \end{array}$$

12
$$\begin{array}{r} 39 \\ +45 \\ \hline 84 \end{array}$$

13
$$\begin{array}{r} 87 \\ -19 \\ \hline \end{array}$$

14
$$\begin{array}{r} 100 \\ - 64 \\ \hline \end{array}$$

15
$$\begin{array}{r} 70 \\ -38 \\ \hline \end{array}$$

1 Write the number that is shown by the drawing.

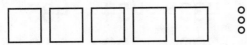

| Hundreds | Tens | Ones | Total |

2 Ming has some baseball cards. He gives 210 of them away. Now he has 323 cards. How many baseball cards did Ming have to start? Circle the number to complete the sentence.

Ming had
| 113 |
| 503 | cards to start.
| 533 |

3 Is this a way to show 613? Choose Yes or No.

| 6 + 1 + 3 | ○ Yes | ○ No |

| 600 + 10 + 3 | ○ Yes | ○ No |

| six hundred thirty-one | ○ Yes | ○ No |

| six hundred thirteen | ○ Yes | ○ No |

4 Claudia has 36 rocks in her collection. She has 49 fewer rocks than Luisa. How many rocks does Luisa have in her collection?

Show your work.

_____ label

5 Choose the ways that show counting by 10s.

- ○ 430 431 432 433 434 435 436 437
- ○ 260 270 280 290 300 310 320 330
- ○ 200 300 400 500 600 700 800 900
- ○ 510 520 530 540 550 560 570 580
- ○ 930 940 950 960 970 980 990 1,000

6 Count by 100s. Write the numbers.

300 400 ____ ____ ____ ____ ____

7 The Nature Club made a 4-page flyer of nature photos.
They want to print 100 copies of the flyer. They have
258 sheets of paper. They buy a pack of 200 sheets.
Do they have enough paper to print the flyers? Explain.

_____

_____

The club adds one more page of photos to each flyer.
Do they have enough paper to print them now? Explain.

_____

_____

8 Match the numbers to <, =, or >.

461 ⑦ 416 •   • =

324 ⊜ 324 •   • <

692 ⑤ 902 •   • >

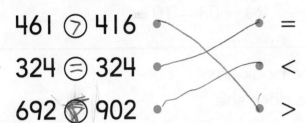

9 Lacey has some coins in her coin collection.
Then her grandmother gives her 252 coins.
Now she has 526 coins. How many coins did
she have to start?

[   ] _____
        label

10 Add. Then choose Yes or No about what you did.

     5 7 4
   + 3 2 6

Make a new ten?   ○ Yes   ○ No

Make a new hundred?   ○ Yes   ○ No

Make a new thousand?   ○ Yes   ○ No

11 Samira has 285 beads. 96 of them are red. The   Show your work.
rest of the beads are blue. How many blue beads
does Samira have?

[   ] _____
        label

Solve.

12 596 − 100 = _____

13 603 − 10 = _____

14 Ada read 124 pages in a book. The book has
300 pages. How many more pages does she
still have to read to finish the book?

Make a drawing. Write an equation.
Solve the problem.

[ ] _____
        label

15 Show and explain how to subtract 279 from 458.
Use the words *hundreds*, *tens*, and *ones*. Explain
how and why you can use addition to check your answer.

_____

_____

_____

_____

_____

Name _____

Boxes of Marbles

Solve and check. Use place value.
Show your work.

Celia and Anthony collect marbles.

```
┌─────────────────────┐        ┌─────────────────────┐
│                     │        │                     │
│  Celia's Marbles    │        │  Anthony's Marbles  │
│       167           │        │        176          │
│                     │        │                     │
└─────────────────────┘        └─────────────────────┘
```

1 Do Celia and Anthony have the same number
of marbles? How do you know?

_____

_____

_____

2 To play a game, Celia and Anthony must first put their
marbles in bags of 10.

How many bags of 10 marbles can Celia fill? ☐

How many bags of 10 marbles can Anthony fill? ☐

If they put their marbles together first, can they fill
the same total number of bags? Explain.

_____

_____

_____

_____

3 Celia buys 16 new marbles. How many marbles
does she have now? How does Celia's new number
of marbles compare with the number of marbles
Anthony has?

_____

_____

_____

4 Anthony wants to have 200 marbles in all. How many
more marbles does he need? Tell how you solved
the problem.

_____

_____

_____

_____

5 Explain how you could use addition or subtraction to
check your answers in problems 3 and 4.

_____

_____

_____

_____

Dear Family:

In this unit, your child will learn about rectangular arrays and how to use addition to count the number of objects in an array. The array below has 2 rows and 3 columns. It can be described as 2 rows with 3 tiles in each row, or 3 columns with 2 tiles in each column.

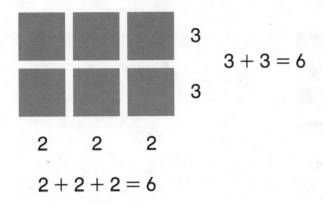

$3 + 3 = 6$

$2 + 2 + 2 = 6$

You can help your child by working with him or her to practice using the words *array*, *rows*, and *columns*. For example, ask your child to use pennies or other small objects to make an array that has 4 rows with 5 objects in each row. Ask your child to write the addition equations that show the total number of objects in the array. ($5 + 5 + 5 + 5 = 20$ and $4 + 4 + 4 + 4 + 4 = 20$)

Your child will also be learning about equal parts of circles and rectangles: 2 *halves*, 3 *thirds*, and 4 *fourths*. You can practice using this vocabulary at home. For example, "I am cutting this pizza into 4 fourths."

Please contact me if you have any questions or concerns.

Sincerely,
Your child's teacher

CC SS Unit 7 addresses the following standards from the Common Core State Standards for Mathematics: **2.OA.A.1**, **2.OA.C.3**, **2.OA.C.4**, **2.NBT.B.5**, **2.NBT.B.6**, **2.MD.A.1**, **2.MD.B.5**, **2.MD.B.6**, **2.G.A.1**, **2.G.A.2**, **2.G.A.3**, and all Mathematical Practices.

Estimada familia:

En esta unidad, su niño aprenderá acerca de las matrices rectangulares y aprenderá cómo usar la suma para contar el número de objetos en una matriz. La matriz de abajo tiene 2 hileras y 3 columnas. Puede describirse así: 2 hileras con 3 fichas en cada columna, o 3 columnas con 2 fichas en cada columna.

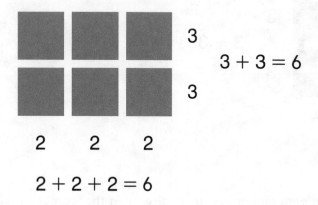

Usted puede ayudar a su niño practicando el uso de las palabras *matriz, hileras* y *columnas*. Por ejemplo, pídale que use monedas de un centavo u otros objetos pequeños para hacer una matriz que tenga 4 hileras con 5 objetos en cada una. Pida a su niño que escriba la ecuación de suma que muestra el número total de objetos en la matriz.
(5 + 5 + 5 + 5 = 20 y 4 + 4 + 4 + 4 + 4 = 20)

Su niño también aprenderá acerca de partes iguales de círculos y rectángulos: 2 *medios,* 3 *tercios* y 4 *cuartos.* Pueden practicar usando este vocabulario en casa. Por ejemplo: "Estoy cortando esta pizza en 4 cuartos."

Si tiene alguna duda o algún comentario, por favor comuníquese conmigo.

Atentamente,
El maestro de su niño

En la Unidad 7 se aplican los siguientes estándares de los Estándares estatales comunes de matemáticas: **2.OA.A.1, 2.OA.C.3, 2.OA.C.4, 2.NBT.B.5, 2.NBT.B.6, 2.MD.A.1, 2.MD.B.5, 2.MD.B.6, 2.G.A.1, 2.G.A.2, 2.G.A.3 y todos los de** Prácticas matemáticas.

array

fourths

columns

halves

equal shares

rows

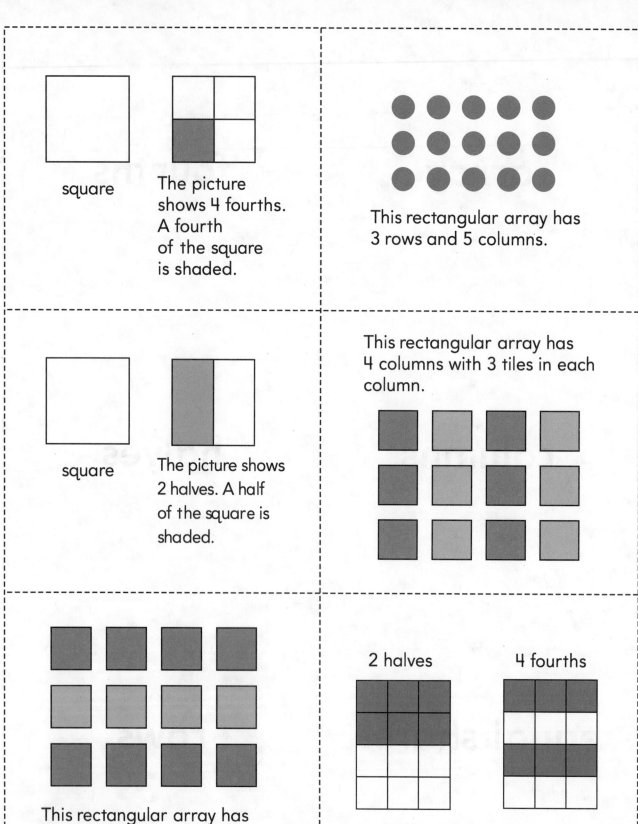

square

The picture shows 4 fourths. A fourth of the square is shaded.

This rectangular array has 3 rows and 5 columns.

square

The picture shows 2 halves. A half of the square is shaded.

This rectangular array has 4 columns with 3 tiles in each column.

This rectangular array has 3 rows with 4 tiles in each row.

2 halves   4 fourths

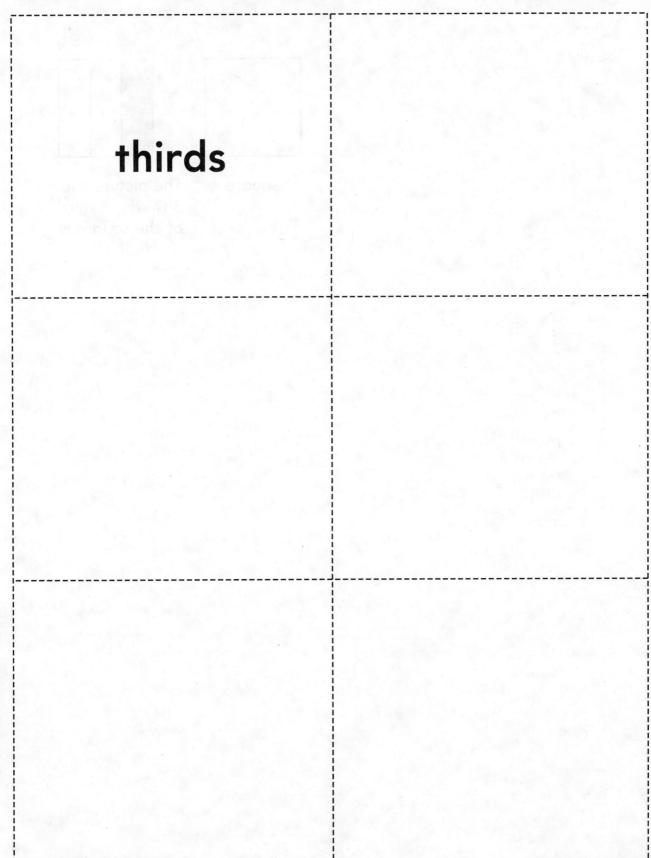

thirds

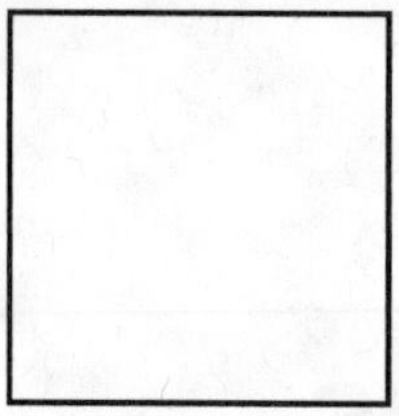

square

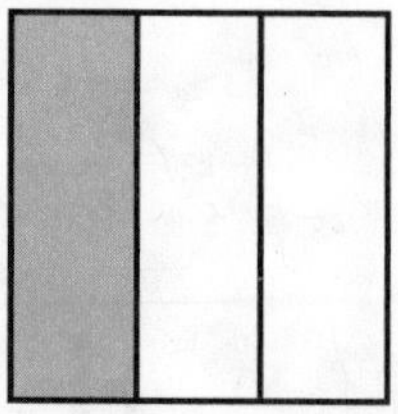

The picture shows 3 thirds. A third of the square is shaded.

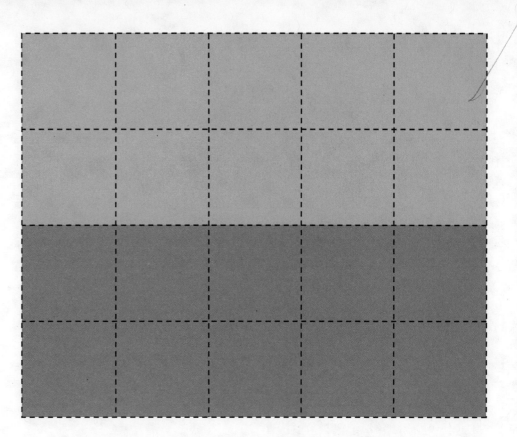

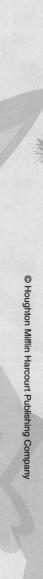

Square-Inch Tiles

Name _____

Rows and Columns

1 Circle the **rows**.

2 Circle the **columns**.

Write Equations for Arrays

Write how many in each row and in each column.
Then write two equations for each **array**.

3

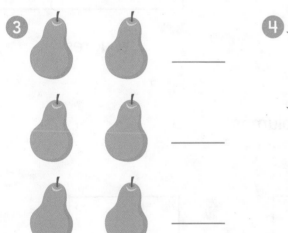

_____

_____

_____

_____   _____

_____

_____

4

_____

_____

_____ _____ _____ _____

_____

_____

Measure to Partition Rectangles

Measure in inches. Draw rows and columns.
Write the number of small squares.

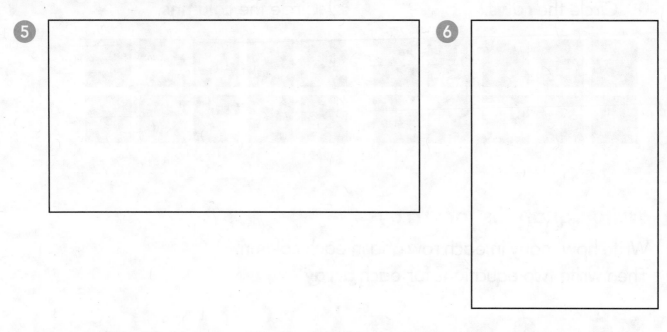

⑤ _____ squares

⑥ _____ squares

Measure in centimeters. Draw rows and columns.
Write the number of small squares.

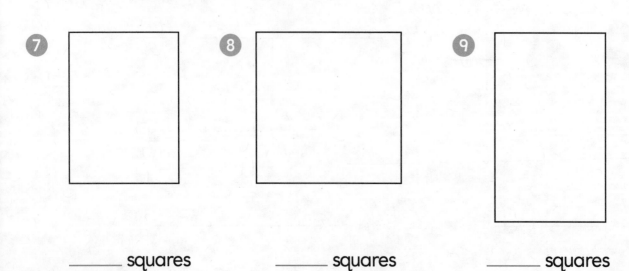

⑦ _____ squares

⑧ _____ squares

⑨ _____ squares

Arrays, Partitioned Rectangles, and Equal Shares

Name _____

Shade Equal Shares

Measure in centimeters. Draw rows and columns.
Shade to show **halves**, **thirds**, and **fourths**.

10 halves

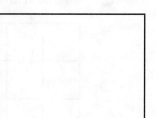

11 thirds

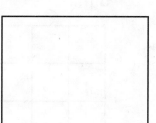

12 fourths

Measure in centimeters. Draw rows and columns.

13 Shade to show halves two different ways.

14 Shade to show fourths two different ways.

15 Shade to show halves two different ways.

Arrays, Partitioned Rectangles, and Equal Shares **371**

More Practice with Equal Shares and Partitions

VOCABULARY
equal shares

Shade to show **equal shares**.

16 2 halves

17 3 thirds

18 4 fourths

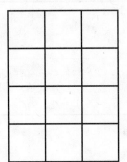

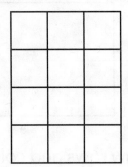

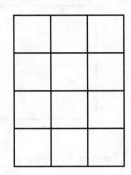

Measure in centimeters. Draw rows and columns.
Write the number of small squares.

19

20

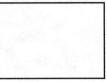

21

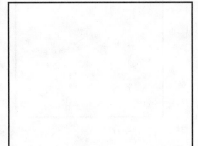

_____ squares

_____ squares

_____ squares

22

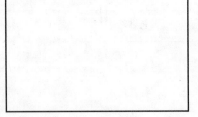

✔ **Check Understanding**

Explain one way to use addition to find the number of objects in the array for Exercise 22.

_____ squares

Arrays, Partitioned Rectangles, and Equal Shares

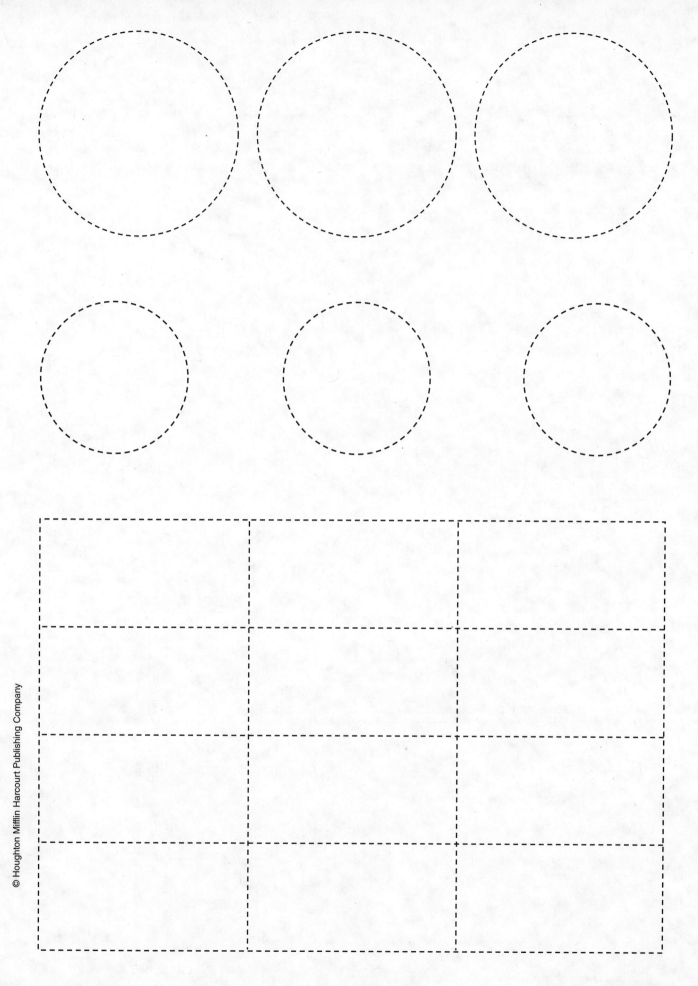

Find Equal Shares

Name _____

Different Shapes of a Half of the Same Rectangle

1 Make two halves. Show different ways.
Shade half of each rectangle.

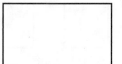 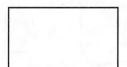 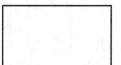 

Different Shapes of a Third of the Same Rectangle

2 Make three thirds. Show different ways.
Shade a third of each rectangle.

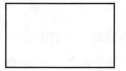 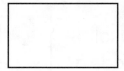  

Different Shapes of a Fourth of the Same Rectangle

3 Make four fourths. Show different ways.
Shade a fourth of each rectangle.

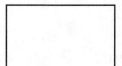   

Equal Shares Using the Same Square

4 Make 2 equal shares. Show different ways. Shade half of each square.

5 Make 3 equal shares. Show different ways. Shade a third of each square.

6 Make 4 equal shares. Show different ways. Shade a fourth of each square.

Equal Shares Using the Same Circle

7 Make 2 equal shares. Shade half of the circle.

8 Make 3 equal shares. Shade a third of the circle.

9 Make 4 equal shares. Shade a fourth of the circle.

Different Shape but Same Size

10 Use Drawings 1, 2, and 3 to explain why the blue and yellow shares are equal.

1   2   3

 Check Understanding

Fill in the blanks to correctly complete the statement.

I know equal shares are the same shape if I can place one share exactly on ____ of another share. I might have to rotate or ____ the share.

Find Equal Shares

Name _____   Date _____

Write how many in each row and in each column.
Then write two addition equations for the array.

1

☆ ☆ ☆ ☆ ☆   _____
☆ ☆ ☆ ☆ ☆   _____
☆ ☆ ☆ ☆ ☆   _____

_____ _____ _____ _____ _____

_____

_____

Measure in centimeters. Draw rows and columns.
Write the number of small squares.

2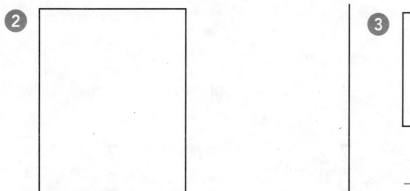

_____ squares

3

_____ squares

Make two halves. Show different ways.

4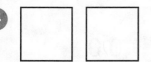

Shade half of the circle.

5

Name _____ **Date** _____

Add or subtract.

1 $7 + 7 = \boxed{}$

2 $8 + 9 = \boxed{}$

3 $12 + 6 = \boxed{}$

4 $11 - 8 = \boxed{}$

5 $16 - 8 = \boxed{}$

6 $13 - 7 = \boxed{}$

7
$$\begin{array}{r} 45 \\ +47 \\ \hline \end{array}$$

8
$$\begin{array}{r} 21 \\ +35 \\ \hline \end{array}$$

9
$$\begin{array}{r} 53 \\ +28 \\ \hline \end{array}$$

10
$$\begin{array}{r} 42 \\ -31 \\ \hline \end{array}$$

11
$$\begin{array}{r} 72 \\ -34 \\ \hline \end{array}$$

12
$$\begin{array}{r} 57 \\ -18 \\ \hline \end{array}$$

13
$$\begin{array}{r} 87 \\ -78 \\ \hline \end{array}$$

14
$$\begin{array}{r} 91 \\ -72 \\ \hline \end{array}$$

15
$$\begin{array}{r} 100 \\ -43 \\ \hline \end{array}$$

Name _____

Solve and Discuss

Solve.   **Show your work.**

① Carl draws a line segment that is 18 centimeters long.
Then he makes it 14 centimeters longer. How long
is the line segment now?

□ _____
        unit

② Samantha runs 45 meters, stops, then runs some more.
She runs a total of 95 meters. How many meters does
she run after her stop?

□ _____
        unit

③ A ribbon is 48 inches long. Taylor uses 32 inches of the
ribbon to make a bow. How much ribbon is left?

□ _____
        unit

④ Mr. Parker cut 9 feet from the end of a pole. The pole
is now 22 feet long. How long was the pole before
Mr. Parker cut it?

□ _____
        unit

Solve and Discuss (continued)

Solve.   **Show your work.**

5 A race course is 99 meters long. There are trees along 38 meters of the course. How long is the part of the course without trees?

[ ] _____
        unit

6 Ms. Godwin paints a fence that is 81 feet long. Mr. Sendak paints a fence that is 56 feet long. How much longer is the fence Ms. Godwin paints?

[ ] _____
        unit

7 O'Shanti has a necklace that is 24 centimeters long. She makes the necklace 36 centimeters longer. How long is the necklace now?

[ ] _____
        unit

8 A giant flag is 6 meters long. Vern adds 4 meters to its length. How long is the flag now?

[ ] _____
        unit

Solve and Discuss (continued)

Solve.

Show your work.

9 Kelly has a piece of red yarn that is 25 centimeters long. She also has a piece of blue yarn that is 11 centimeters long. How much longer is the red yarn than the blue yarn?

☐ _____
  unit

10 Paco swims 41 meters. Kenny swims 4 meters less than Paco. How far does Kenny swim?

☐ _____
  unit

11 Leonard walks 28 meters. Then he walks 56 more meters. How many meters does he walk in all?

☐ _____
  unit

12 A tree is 72 inches tall now. It is 12 inches taller than it was last year. How tall was the tree last year?

☐ _____
  unit

Number Line Diagrams

Use the number line diagram to add or subtract.

13 Loop 17 and 28. Loop the difference *D*.

How long is it? _____

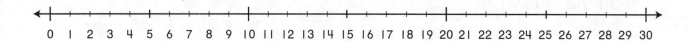

14 Loop 17 and 35. Loop the difference *D*.

How long is it? _____

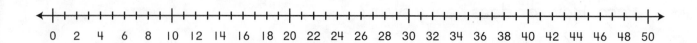

15 Loop 38 and 84. Loop the difference *D*.

How long is it? _____

16 Loop 67. Add 26 to it. Loop the total *T*.

How long is it? _____

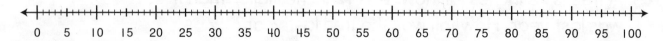

✓ **Check Understanding**

Explain how solving a length word problem is different from solving other word problems.

　　　　Length Word Problems and Number Line Diagrams

Name _____

Lengths at the Grocery Store

Choose a method to solve the problems. Does your method work for all of them? Be ready to explain your method to the class.

---

1 Someone spills a carton of juice in the store. Mr. Green cleans it up. Then he blocks off the wet spot with tape. How long is the tape?

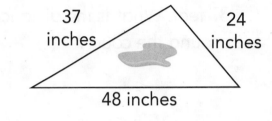

37 inches

24 inches

48 inches

[_____] _____
               unit

---

2 Mrs. Chang wants to decorate the table she uses for free food samples. She wants to put gold trim around the top of the table. How much trim will she need?

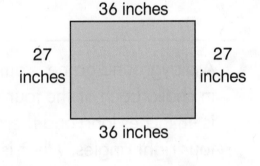

36 inches

27 inches

27 inches

36 inches

[_____] _____
               unit

---

3 Here is the route a customer takes while shopping at the store. How far does the customer walk altogether?

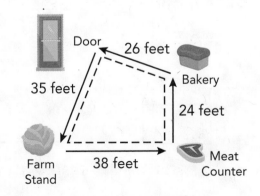

Door   26 feet

35 feet

Bakery

24 feet

Farm Stand   38 feet   Meat Counter

[_____] _____
               unit

Playground Lengths

Solve.   **Show your work.**

④ The basketball court has four right angles and sides that are 42 feet, 37 feet, 42 feet, and 37 feet. What is the distance around the court?

☐ _____
        unit

⑤ The fence around the picnic area has sides with lengths of 33 yards, 56 yards, and 61 yards. What is the total length of the fence?

☐ _____
        unit

⑥ A playground game is outlined in chalk. Each of the four sides is 48 inches long and there are four right angles. What is the total length of the outline?

☐ _____
        unit

⑦ The play area has a wood border. The border has sides that are 32 feet, 45 feet, 29 feet, and 61 feet. What is distance around the play area?

☐ _____
        unit

Add Three and Four Lengths

Name _____

Distance Around Shapes at Home

Solve.

Show your work.

---

8 A border outlines a flower bed. How long is the border?

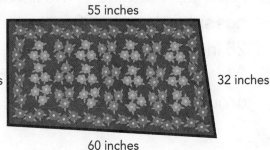

55 inches

29 inches   32 inches

60 inches

```
┌──────────┐
│          │   _____
└──────────┘        unit
```

---

9 The pantry has a tiled floor. What is the distance around the tiled floor?

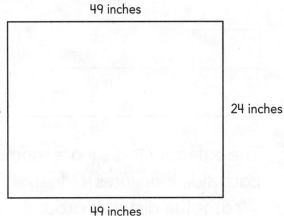

49 inches

24 inches   24 inches

49 inches

```
┌──────────┐
│          │   _____
└──────────┘        unit
```

---

10 In spring, all of the wood floors get waxed. This part of the library floor was waxed. What is the distance around the waxed part?

13 feet   12 feet

21 feet

```
┌──────────┐
│          │   _____
└──────────┘        unit
```

Distance Around Shapes at School

Solve.   **Show your work.**

⓫ A picture hanging in the library has sides that are 39 inches, 28 inches, 39 inches, and 28 inches. What is the distance around the picture?

```
┌──────┐
│      │ _____
└──────┘    unit
```

⓬ The second grade class makes an art project. The lengths of the sides of the project are 18 inches, 24 inches, and 19 inches. The teacher wants to frame the project with tape. How much tape does she need?

```
┌──────┐
│      │ _____
└──────┘    unit
```

⓭ The cafeteria is a square room. Each side measures 47 feet. What is the distance around the room?

```
┌──────┐
│      │ _____
└──────┘    unit
```

⓮ The school patio has 4 sides. The lengths of the sides are 22 feet, 18 feet, 27 feet, and 16 feet. What is the distance around the patio?

```
┌──────┐
│      │ _____
└──────┘    unit
```

 Check Understanding

Draw to show the method you used to add the three numbers in Problem 12.

Add Three and Four Lengths

Solve and Discuss

Solve.

Show your work.

1 Miss Springfield is building shelves. The bottom shelf is 64 inches long. The top shelf is 27 inches longer than the bottom shelf. How long is the top shelf?

_____

2 The top of a bookcase is 24 inches from the ceiling. The ceiling is 96 inches tall. How tall is the bookcase?

_____

3 Mr. Tracy is putting a border of rocks around his garden. The lengths of the sides of the garden are 12 feet, 19 feet, and 27 feet. How long will the border be?

_____

4 Brendan is knitting a scarf. It is 28 centimeters long. Then he knits 18 centimeters more. How long is the scarf now?

_____

CC SS Content Standards **2.OA.A.1, 2.NBT.B.5, 2.NBT.B.6, 2.MD.B.5, 2.MD.B.6**
Mathematical Practices **MP1, MP2, MP3, MP6**

More Length Word Problems **387**

Length Word Problems

Solve.   **Show your work.**

5 Hannah has a red ribbon and a blue ribbon. The red ribbon
is 17 cm long. The blue ribbon is 13 cm long. How much
longer is the red ribbon than the blue ribbon?

_____

6 A roll of tape is 76 feet long to start. Mr. Novak uses 24 feet
of the tape. How much tape is left?

_____

7 Nick and Ben are running a relay race. Nick runs 48 meters.
Ben runs 37 meters. How many fewer meters does Ben run?

_____

8 Mrs. Rossi is putting a fence around her garden. The
garden has 4 sides and 4 right angles. Each side of the
garden is 23 feet long. How long will the fence be?

_____

More Length Word Problems

Length Word Problems (continued)

Solve.   Show your work.

9 Caroline uses tape to mark off the space where new grass was
planted. The lengths of the sides of the space are 16 feet,
28 feet, 36 feet, and 18 feet. How much tape is needed?

_____

10 Mr. Morris pulls the shade down. It covers 24 inches of the
window. Mrs. Morris pulls it down 48 more inches. What is the
length of the shade now?

_____

11 A flagpole is 62 feet tall. The flag covers 11 feet of the pole.
How long is the part not covered by the flag?

_____

12 Miguel is putting a string of lights around a sign. The lengths of
the sides of the sign are 26 inches, 18 inches, 26 inches, and
18 inches. What length of lights does he need?

_____

✓ **Check Understanding**
What shape is the sign in Problem 12? Circle your answer.

square   rectangle   triangle

What's the Error?

$$57 + 29 = \boxed{}$$

I'm trying to add 57 and 29. I'm not sure what to do next.

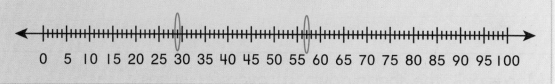

0 5 10 15 20 25 30 35 40 45 50 55 60 65 70 75 80 85 90 95 100

⑬ Show how to use the number line diagram to find the total.

$$57 + 29 = \boxed{}$$

0 5 10 15 20 25 30 35 40 45 50 55 60 65 70 75 80 85 90 95 100

Number Line Diagrams

Represent each equation on the number line diagram.
Then find the difference or the total.

⑭ $43 + \boxed{} = 72$

0 5 10 15 20 25 30 35 40 45 50 55 60 65 70 75 80 85 90 95 100

⑮ $\boxed{} + 28 = 86$

0 5 10 15 20 25 30 35 40 45 50 55 60 65 70 75 80 85 90 95 100

More Length Word Problems

Name _____

Flags with Equal Parts

Ships can use flags to send messages. A flag can be used alone to send a message. A group of flags can be used to spell out a message.

This flag means "I have a pilot on board." It can also be used for the letter H.

1. How many parts does the flag have?

   _____ parts

2. Does the flag show equal parts?

   yes   no

This flag means "Return to ship." It can also be used for the letter P.

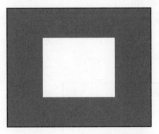

3. How many parts does the flag have?

   _____ parts

4. Does the flag show equal parts?

   yes   no

CCSS Content Standards **2.G.A.3**
Mathematical Practices **MP1, MP3, MP5, MP6, MP8**

Square Flags

5 Draw a square flag. Show halves. Color the flag. Color a half of the flag blue.

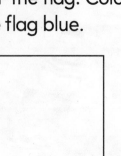

6 Draw a square flag. Show thirds. Color the flag. Color a third of the flag red.

Rectangular Flags

7 Show 4 equal shares that are rectangles.

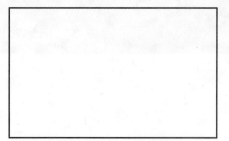

8 Show 4 equal shares that are triangles.

9 On a separate sheet of paper, design your own flag. Use equal parts. Color your flag.

Focus on Mathematical Practices

Show the equation on the number line diagram.
Then find the difference or the total.

1 48 + 31 = ☐

⟵|ıı|ıı|ıı|ıı|ıı|ıı|ıı|ıı|ıı|ıı|ıı|ıı|ıı|ıı|ıı|ıı|ıı|ıı|ıı|ıı|⟶
0   5 10 15 20 25 30 35 40 45 50 55 60 65 70 75 80 85 90 95 100

2 44 + ☐ = 62

⟵|ıı|ıı|ıı|ıı|ıı|ıı|ıı|ıı|ıı|ıı|ıı|ıı|ıı|ıı|ıı|ıı|ıı|ıı|ıı|ıı|⟶
0   5 10 15 20 25 30 35 40 45 50 55 60 65 70 75 80 85 90 95 100

Solve.   Show your work.

3 Marissa wants to decorate a table for a party.
She wants to put silver trim around the top
of the table. How much trim will she need?

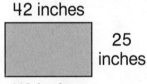

42 inches

25 inches   25 inches

42 inches

☐ _____
        unit

4 A ribbon is 54 inches long. Grace uses
41 inches of the ribbon to make a gift.
How much ribbon is left?

☐ _____
        unit

5 The red rope is 64 feet long. The yellow
rope is 39 feet. How many feet shorter
is the yellow rope?

☐ _____
        unit

Name _____ **Date** _____

Add or subtract.

1 $15 - 4 = \boxed{}$ **2** $15 - 12 = \boxed{}$ **3** $18 - 10 = \boxed{}$

4 $9 + 8 = \boxed{}$ **5** $12 + 6 = \boxed{}$ **6** $13 + 7 = \boxed{}$

7
$$\begin{array}{r} 34 \\ -\ 3 \\ \hline \end{array}$$

8
$$\begin{array}{r} 45 \\ -19 \\ \hline \end{array}$$

9
$$\begin{array}{r} 64 \\ -29 \\ \hline \end{array}$$

10
$$\begin{array}{r} 28 \\ +41 \\ \hline \end{array}$$

11
$$\begin{array}{r} 36 \\ +46 \\ \hline \end{array}$$

12
$$\begin{array}{r} 58 \\ +14 \\ \hline \end{array}$$

13
$$\begin{array}{r} 90 \\ -12 \\ \hline \end{array}$$

14
$$\begin{array}{r} 95 \\ -69 \\ \hline \end{array}$$

15
$$\begin{array}{r} 94 \\ -67 \\ \hline \end{array}$$

1 Write how many in each row and in each column.

_____

_____

_____

_____

_____ _____ _____

2 Does the equation match the array above?
Choose Yes or No.

$3 + 3 + 3 = 9$ ○ Yes   ○ No

$4 + 4 + 4 = 12$ ○ Yes   ○ No

$3 + 3 + 3 + 3 = 12$ ○ Yes   ○ No

$4 + 4 + 4 + 4 = 16$ ○ Yes   ○ No

3 Measure in centimeters.
Draw rows and columns. Write
the number of small squares.

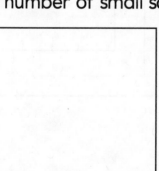

_____ squares

4 Measure in inches.
Draw rows and columns. Write
the number of small squares.

_____ squares

5 Look at these shapes.

Are the shaded parts the same shape? Explain.

_____

Are the shaded parts the same size? Explain.

_____

_____

6 Draw lines in each shape to make equal shares.

Two Halves	Three Thirds	Four Fourths
◯	◯	◯
▭	▭	▭

7 Choose the squares that show a third shaded.

  ◯   ◯   ◯   ◯   ◯

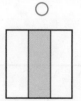   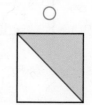

Solve. Circle the number to complete the sentence.

8 Jennifer has 66 inches of red yarn. She has
14 more inches of blue yarn than red yarn. How
many inches of blue yarn does Jennifer have?

Jennifer has
| 70 |
| 80 |
| 90 |
inches of blue yarn.

9 Elizabeth is shoveling snow from a sidewalk
that is 20 feet long. So far she has shoveled
6 feet of the sidewalk. How many more feet
does she need to shovel?

Elizabeth needs to shovel
| 14 |
| 16 |
| 26 |
more feet.

Write an equation and solve.

10 Jake is using fencing to make a dog pen. The pen has three sides. Two
sides are 6 feet long. The third side is 3 feet long. How many feet of
fencing does Jake need?

_____ = ☐ _____
                    unit

11 Devon uses gold ribbon to make a border
around a square picture. Each side of the
picture is 14 centimeters long. How many
centimeters of gold ribbon does Devon need?

_____ = ☐ _____
                    unit

12 Write a term from a tile to tell how much is shaded.

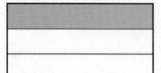 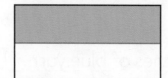 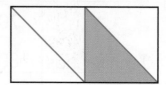

_____ _____ _____

13 Complete the equation that the number line diagram represents.

0 5 10 15 20 25 30 35 40 45 50 55 60 65 70 75 80 85 90 95 100

☐ + 15 = ☐

14 Represent the equation on the number line diagram.

$46 + 21 =$

0   5   10 15 20 25 30 35 40 45 50 55 60 65 70 75 80 85 90 95 100

Find the total.

$46 + 21 =$ ☐

Marching Band

1 The 8 drummers in a marching band line up in equal rows. Show one way they could line up. Shade a ☐ to show each drummer.

2 Show a different way the 8 drummers could line up in equal rows.

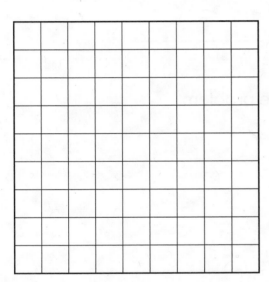

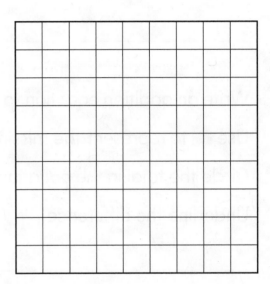

3 Write an addition equation for each array.

_____

_____

4 Half of the drummers go home. Can the remaining drummers still line up in equal rows? Explain your thinking.

_____

_____

There are 60 students in the marching band.
Eight students are drummers. Five students play the flute.
How many students in the band do not play the drum
or flute?

5 Explain how you would solve the problem.

_____

_____

_____

6 Write an addition equation to solve the problem.

Use ▮ to represent the missing number.

Circle the total in the equation.

Underline the difference.

_____

7 Show the equation on the number line diagram.

Then write the answer.

```
<———|||||||||||||||||||||||||||||||||||||||||||||||||||||||||———>
    0   5  10  15  20  25  30  35  40  45  50  55  60  65  70  75  80  85  90  95  100
```

[ ] students do not play the drum or flute.

	Result Unknown	Change Unknown	Start Unknown
Add To	Aisha has 46 stamps in her collection. Then her grandfather gives her 29 stamps. How many stamps does she have now? *Situation and Solution Equation:* $46 + 29 = \square$	Aisha has 46 stamps in her collection. Then her grandfather gives her some stamps. Now she has 75 stamps. How many stamps did her grandfather give her? *Situation Equation:* $46 + \square = 75$ *Solution Equation:* $\square = 75 - 46$	Aisha has some stamps in her collection. Then her grandfather gives her 29 stamps. Now she has 75 stamps. How many stamps did she have to start? *Situation Equation:* $\square + 29 = 75$ *Solution Equation:* $\square = 75 - 29$
Take From	A store has 43 bottles of water at the start of the day. During the day, the store sells 25 bottles. How many bottles do they have at the end of the day? *Situation and Solution Equation:* $43 - 25 = \square$	A store has 43 bottles of water at the start of the day. The store has 18 bottles left at the end of the day. How many bottles does the store sell? *Situation Equation:* $43 - \square = 18$ *Solution Equation:* $\square = 43 - 18$	A store sells 25 bottles of water during one day. At the end of the day 18 bottles are left. How many bottles did the store have at the beginning of the day? *Situation Equation:* $\square - 25 = 18$ *Solution Equation:* $\square = 25 + 18$

[1]A situation equation represents the structure (action) in the problem situation. A solution equation shows the operation used to find the answer.

Problem Types

	Total Unknown	Addend Unknown	Both Addends Unknown
Put Together/ Take Apart	A clothing store has 39 shirts with short sleeves and 45 shirts with long sleeves. How many shirts does the store have in all? *Math Drawing[2]:* 39 45 *Situation and Solution Equation:* $39 + 45 = \square$	Of the 84 shirts in a clothing store, 39 have short sleeves. The rest have long sleeves. How many shirts have long sleeves? *Math Drawing:* 84 39 *Situation Equation:* $84 = 39 + \square$ *Solution Equation:* $84 - 39 = \square$	Pam has 24 roses. How many can she put in her red vase and how many in her blue vase? *Math Drawing:* 24 *Situation Equation:* $24 = \square + \square$

[2]These math drawings are called Math Mountains in Grades 1–3 and break-apart drawings in Grades 4 and 5.

	Difference Unknown	Greater Unknown	Smaller Unknown
Compare[1]	Alex has 64 trading cards. Lucy has 48 trading cards. How many more trading cards does Alex have than Lucy? Lucy has 48 trading cards. Alex has 64 trading cards. How many fewer trading cards does Lucy have than Alex? *Math Drawing:* A ▭ 64 L ▭ 48 ⬭ ? *Situation Equation:* $48 + \square = 64$ or $\square = 64 - 48$ *Solution Equation:* $\square = 64 - 48$	**Leading Language** Lucy has 48 trading cards. Alex has 16 more trading cards than Lucy. How many trading cards does Alex have? **Misleading Language** Lucy has 48 trading cards. Lucy has 16 fewer trading cards than Alex. How many trading cards does Alex have? *Math Drawing:* A ▭ ? L ▭ 48 ⬭ 16 *Situation and Solution Equation:* $48 + 16 = \square$	**Leading Language** Alex has 64 trading cards. Lucy has 16 fewer trading cards than Alex. How many trading cards does Lucy have? **Misleading Language** Alex has 64 trading cards. Alex has 16 more trading cards than Lucy. How many trading cards does Lucy have? *Math Drawing:* A ▭ 64 L ▭ ? ⬭ 16 *Situation Equation:* $\square + 16 = 64$ or $\square = 64 - 16$ *Solution Equation:* $\square = 64 - 16$

[1]A comparison sentence can always be said in two ways. One way uses *more*, and the other uses *fewer* or *less*. Misleading language suggests the wrong operation. For example, it says *Lucy has 16 fewer trading cards than Alex*, but you have to add 16 cards to the number of cards Lucy has to get the number of cards Alex has.

Glossary

5-groups*

||||| ||||| tens in 5-groups

○○○○○ ones in 5-groups
○○○○○

add

$$4 + 2 = 6$$

addend

$$5 + 6 = 11$$

↑ ↑

addends

Adding Up Method* (for Subtraction)

$$\begin{array}{r} 144 \\ -\ 68 \\ \hline 76 \end{array}$$

$$68 + 2 = 70$$
$$70 + 30 = 100$$
$$\underline{100 + 44 = 114}$$
$$\boxed{76}$$

addition doubles*

Both addends (or partners) are the same.

$$4 + 4 = 8$$

A.M.

Use A.M. for times between midnight and noon.

analog clock

angle

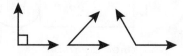

These are angles.

array

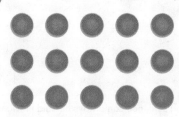

This rectangular array has 3 rows and 5 columns.

*A classroom research-based term developed for *Math Expressions*

B

bar graph

Coins in My Collection

horizontal bar graph

Flowers in My Garden

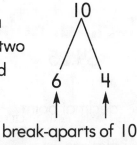

vertical bar graph

break-apart*

You can break apart a larger number to get two smaller amounts called break-aparts.

break-aparts of 10

C

cent

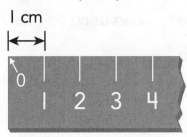

front   back

1 cent or 1¢ or $0.01

centimeter (cm)

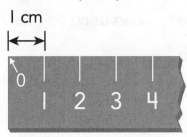

cent sign

56¢

↑

cent sign

clock

analog clock

digital clock

columns

This rectangular array has 4 columns with 3 tiles in each column.

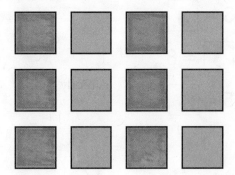

*A classroom research-based term developed for *Math Expressions*

Glossary

compare numbers

Compare numbers using >, <, or =.

$52 > 25$

$25 < 52$

$25 = 25$

comparison bars*

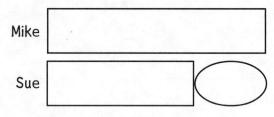

You can add labels and fill in numbers to help you solve *Compare* problems.

count all*

$5 + 3 = \square$

1 2 3 4 5 6 7 8

● ● ● ● ● ● ● ●

$5 + 3 = 8$

count on

$5 + 3 = 8$

$5 + 3 = 8$

$8 - 5 = 3$

Already **5**

cube

D

data

	Sisters	Brothers
Kendra	2	1
Scott	2	0
Ida	0	1

data

The data in the table show how many sisters and how many brothers each child has.

decade numbers*

10, 20, 30, 40, 50, 60, 70, 80, 90

decimal point

$4.25

decimal point

diagonal

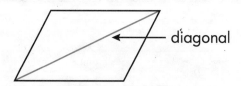

diagonal

*A classroom research-based term developed for *Math Expressions*

difference

$$11 - 3 = 8$$

$$\begin{array}{r} 11 \\ -\ 3 \\ \hline \text{difference} \longrightarrow 8 \end{array}$$

digital clock

digits

0, 1, 2, 3, 4, 5, 6, 7, 8, 9

15 is a 2-digit number.

The 1 in 15 means 1 ten.

The 5 in 15 means 5 ones.

dime

front   back

10 cents or 10¢ or $0.10

dollar

100 cents or

100¢ or $1.00

front

back

dollar sign

$4.25

↑

dollar sign

doubles minus 1

$7 + 7 = 14$, so

$7 + 6 = 13$, 1 less than 14.

doubles minus 2

$7 + 7 = 14$, so

$7 + 5 = 12$, 2 less than 14.

doubles plus 1

$6 + 6 = 12$, so

$6 + 7 = 13$, 1 more than 12.

doubles plus 2

$6 + 6 = 12$, so

$6 + 8 = 14$, 2 more than 12.

E

equal shares

2 halves   4 fourths

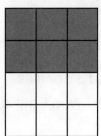   

*A classroom research-based term developed for *Math Expressions*

Glossary

equation

$$4 + 3 = 7 \qquad 7 = 4 + 3$$
$$9 - 5 = 4 \qquad 4 + 5 = 8 + 1$$

An equation must have an $=$ sign.

equation chain*

$$3 + 4 = 5 + 2 = 8 - 1 = 7$$

estimate

Make a reasonable guess about how many or how much.

even

A number is even if you can make groups of 2 and have none left over.

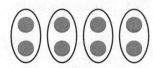

8 is an even number.

exact change

I will pay with 4 dimes and 3 pennies. That is the exact change. I won't get any money back.

expanded form

$$283 = 200 + 80 + 3$$

Expanded Method (for Addition)*

$$
\begin{array}{rcl}
78 & = & 70 + 8 \\
+\,57 & = & 50 + 7 \\
\hline
& & 120 + 15 = 135
\end{array}
$$

Expanded Method* (for Subtraction)

$$
\begin{array}{rcl}
64 & = & \overset{50}{\cancel{60}} + \overset{14}{\cancel{4}} \\
-\,28 & = & 20 + 8 \\
\hline
& & 30 + 6 = 36
\end{array}
$$

extra information

Franny has 8 kittens and 2 dogs. 4 kittens are asleep. How many kittens are awake?

$$8 - 4 = \boxed{4}$$

The number of dogs is extra information. It is not needed to solve the problem.

F

fewer

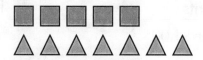

There are fewer ■ than △.

*A classroom research-based term developed for *Math Expressions*

foot (ft)

foot

12 inches = 1 foot   (not drawn to scale)

fourths

square

The picture shows 4 fourths. A fourth of the square is shaded.

greatest

25   41   63

63 is the greatest number.

group name*

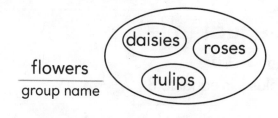

flowers
group name

half hour

5 minutes
10 minutes
15 minutes
20 minutes
25 minutes
30 minutes

30 minutes = 1 half hour

halves

square

The picture shows 2 halves. A half of the square is shaded.

hexagon

A hexagon has 6 sides and 6 angles.

*A classroom research-based term developed for *Math Expressions*

hidden information

Heather bought a dozen eggs. She used 7 of them to make breakfast. How many eggs does she have left?

$$12 - 7 = \boxed{5}$$

The hidden information is that a dozen means 12.

horizontal bar graph

Coins in My Collection

horizontal form

$$4 + 5 = 9$$

horizontal line

hour

60 minutes = 1 hour

hour hand

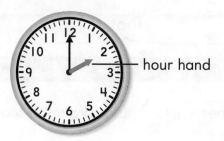

hour hand

hundreds

3 hundreds

347 has 3 hundreds.

↑
hundreds

I

inch (in.)

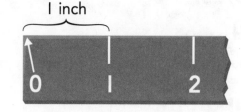

1 inch

is equal to (=)

$$5 + 3 = 8$$

5 plus 3 is equal to 8.

is greater than (>)

34   >   25

34 is greater than 25.

*A classroom research-based term developed for *Math Expressions*

© Houghton Mifflin Harcourt Publishing Company

is less than (<)

45   <   46

45 is less than 46.

L

least

14   7   63

7 is the least number.

length

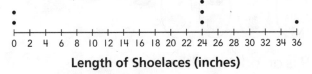

The length of the pencil is about 17 cm.
(not to scale)

line plot

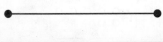
0 2 4 6 8 10 12 14 16 18 20 22 24 26 28 30 32 34 36
Length of Shoelaces (inches)

line segment

●━━━━━━━━━━●

M

make a ten

$8 + 6 = \boxed{}$

8 ●● | ●●●●●
   10 + 4

   10 + 4 = 14,

so 8 + 6 = 14

matching drawing*

 fewer

○○○○○○○ more

Math Mountain*

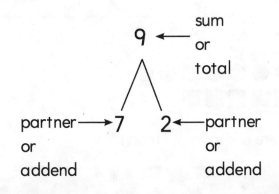

partner   partner
or   or
addend   addend

meter(m)

100 centimeters = 1 meter
(not drawn to scale)

minus

$8 - 3 = 5$

$$\begin{array}{r} 8 \\ -3 \\ \hline 5 \end{array}$$

8 minus 3 equals 5.

minute

60 seconds = 1 minute

*A classroom research-based term developed for *Math Expressions*

Glossary

minute hand

minute hand: points to the minutes

more

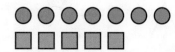

There are more ⬤ than ◻.

New Groups Above Method*

$$\begin{array}{r} \overset{1}{5}6 \\ +\ 28 \\ \hline 84 \end{array}$$

$6 + 8 = 14$

The 1 new ten in 14 goes up to the tens place.

New Groups Below Method*

$$\begin{array}{r} 56 \\ +\ 28 \\ \hline \underset{1}{8}4 \end{array}$$

$6 + 8 = 14$

The 1 new ten in 14 goes below in the tens place.

nickel

front   back

5 cents or 5¢ or $0.05

not equal to (≠)

$$6 + 4 \neq 8$$

$6 + 4$ is not equal to 8.

number line diagram

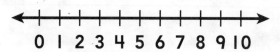

This is a number line diagram.

number name

12

twelve ⟵ number name

odd

A number is odd if you can make groups of 2 and have one left over.

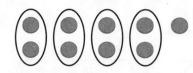

9 is an odd number.

ones

7 ones

347 has 7 ones.

↑

ones

*A classroom research-based term developed for *Math Expressions*

opposite operations

Addition and subtraction are opposite operations.

$$5 + 9 = 14$$
$$14 - 9 = 5$$

Use addition to check subtraction. Use subtraction to check addition.

opposite sides

opposite sides

order

2, 5, 6

The numbers 2, 5, and 6 are in order from least to greatest.

P

pairs

A group of 2 is a pair.

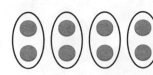

The picture shows 4 pairs of counters.

partner lengths*

partner lengths of 4 cm

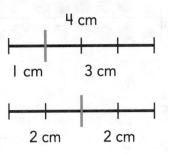

4 cm

1 cm   3 cm

2 cm   2 cm

partners*

$$9 + 6 = 15$$

partners (addends)

pattern

This pattern shows counting by 2s.

2, 4, 6, 8, 10

penny

front   back

1 cent or 1¢ or $0.01

pentagon

A pentagon has 5 sides and 5 angles.

© Houghton Mifflin Harcourt Publishing Company

*A classroom research-based term developed for *Math Expressions*

picture graph

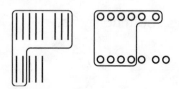

| Apples | 🍎🍎🍎🍎🍎🍎🍎 |
| Oranges | 🟠🟠🟠🟠🟠🟠🟠🟠🟠 |

plus

$3 + 2 = 5$

3 plus 2 equals 5.

$$\begin{array}{r} 3 \\ +2 \\ \hline 5 \end{array}$$

P.M.

Use P.M. for times between noon and midnight.

proof drawing*

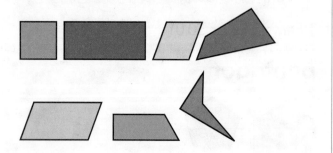

$86 + 57 = 143$

Q

quadrilateral

A quadrilateral has 4 sides and 4 angles.

quarter*

front   back

25 cents or 25¢ or $0.25

A quarter is another name for a fourth.
A quarter is a fourth of a dollar.

quick hundreds*

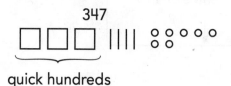

347

quick hundreds

quick tens*

162

quick tens

R

rectangle

A rectangle has 4 sides and 4 right angles.
Opposite sides have the same length.

rectangular prism

---

*A classroom research-based term developed for *Math Expressions*

right angle

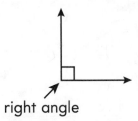

right angle

A right angle is sometimes called a *square corner*.

round

Express a number to the nearest ten or hundred. You can round down or round up.

52 ⟶ 50   278 ⟶ 300

rows

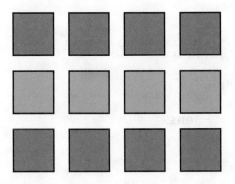

This rectangular array has 3 rows with 4 tiles in each row.

ruler

A ruler is used to measure length.

S

scale

Coins in My Collection

scale

The numbers along the side or the bottom of a graph.

Show All Totals Method*

```
   25            724
 + 48          + 158
 ----          -----
   60            800
   13             70
 ----             12
   73          -----
                 882
```

situation equation*

A baker baked 100 loaves of bread. He sold some loaves. There are 73 loaves left. How many loaves of bread did he sell?

100 − ☐ = 73

situation equation

*A classroom research-based term developed for *Math Expressions*

Glossary

skip count

skip count by 2s: 2, 4, 6, 8, . . .
skip count by 5s: 5, 10, 15, 20, . . .
skip count by 10s: 10, 20, 30, 40, 50, . . .

solution equation*

A baker baked 100 loaves of bread. He sold some loaves. There are 73 loaves left. How many loaves of bread did he sell?

$$100 - 73 = \boxed{}$$

solution equation

square

A square has 4 equal sides and 4 right angles.

subtract

$$8 - 5 = 3$$

subtraction doubles*

The subtrahend and the difference, or partners, are the same.

$$8 - 4 = 4$$

sum

$$4 + 3 = 7$$

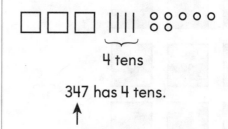

sum →

survey

When you collect data by asking people questions, you are taking a survey.

T

teen number

any number from 11 to 19

11 12 13 14 15 16 17 18 19

tens

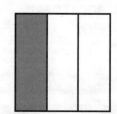

4 tens

347 has 4 tens.

↑
tens

thirds

square

The picture shows 3 thirds. A third of the square is shaded.

© Houghton Mifflin Harcourt Publishing Company

*A classroom research-based term developed for *Math Expressions*

thousand

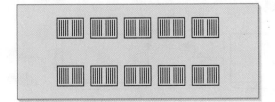

1,000 = ten hundreds

total

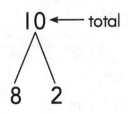

10 ← total

8   2

triangle

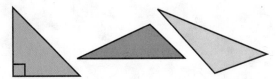

A triangle has 3 sides and 3 angles.

U

ungroup*

Ungroup when you need more ones or tens to subtract.

Ungroup First Method*

6 4
− 2 8
↑ ↑
yes no

1. Check to see if there are enough tens and ones to subtract.

514
6̸ 4̸
− 2 8

2. You can get more ones by taking from the tens and putting them in the ones place.

514
6̸ 4̸
− 2 8
36

3. Subtract from either right to left or left to right.

---

unknown addend

3 + □ = 9
↑
unknown addend

---

unknown total

3 + 6 = □
↑
unknown total

V

vertical form

4
+ 3
7

---

*A classroom research-based term developed for *Math Expressions*

Glossary

vertical bar graph

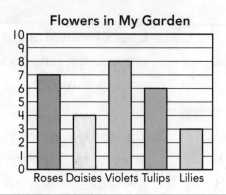

Flowers in My Garden

vertical line

view

This is the side view of the rectangular prism above.

width

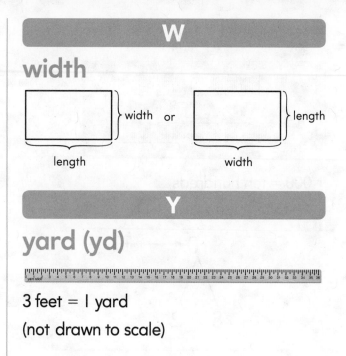

width   or   length

length   width

yard (yd)

3 feet = 1 yard

(not drawn to scale)

*A classroom research-based term developed for *Math Expressions*

2.OA Operations and Algebraic Thinking

Represent and solve problems involving addition and subtraction.

2.OA.A.1	Use addition and subtraction within 100 to solve one-and two-step word problems involving situations of adding to, taking from, putting together, taking apart, and comparing, with unknowns in all positions, e.g., by using drawings and equations with a symbol for the unknown number to represent the problem.	Unit 1 Lessons 1, 2, 4, 10, 11, 12, 13, 14, 15, 16, 17, 18, 19, 20, 21; Unit 2 Lessons 1, 2, 7, 15; Unit 4 Lessons 3, 4, 5, 12, 13, 14, 16, 17, 18, 19, 20, 21, 22, 23; Unit 5 Lessons 3, 4, 5, 6, 7, 9, 10; Unit 6 Lessons 8, 9, 14, 15; Unit 7 Lessons 3, 4, 5

Add and subtract within 20.

2.OA.B.2	Fluently add and subtract within 20 using mental strategies. By end of Grade 2, know from memory all sums of two one-digit numbers.	Unit 1 Lessons 1, 2, 3, 4, 5, 7, 8, 9, 10, 11, 12, 13, 14, 15, 16, 17, 18, 19, 20, 21; Unit 2 Lessons 1, 2, 6; Unit 3 Lessons 1, 2, 3, 4; Unit 4 Lessons 6, 13; Unit 5 Lessons 3, 4, 5, 9, 10

Work with equal groups of objects to gain foundations for multiplication.

2.OA.C.3	Determine whether a group of objects (up to 20) has an odd or even number of members, e.g., by pairing objects or counting them by 2s; write an equation to express an even number as a sum of two equal addends.	Unit 1 Lessons 6, 7, 21; Unit 7 Lesson 1
2.OA.C.4	Use addition to find the total number of objects arranged in rectangular arrays with up to 5 rows and up to 5 columns; write an equation to express the total as a sum of equal addends.	Unit 7 Lessons 1, 6

■ **Major**   ■ **Supporting**   ■ **Additional**

2.NBT Number and Operations in Base Ten

Understand place value.

2.NBT.A.1	Understand that the three digits of a three-digit number represent amounts of hundreds, tens, and ones; e.g., 706 equals 7 hundreds, 0 tens, and 6 ones.	Unit 2 Lessons 1, 2, 3, 4, 5, 6, 7, 8, 9, 10, 11; Unit 4 Lessons 7, 8, 9, 10, 12 ,14; Unit 6 Lesson 2
2.NBT.A.1.a	Understand that the three digits of a three-digit number represent amounts of hundreds, tens, and ones; e.g., 706 equals 7 hundreds, 0 tens, and 6 ones. Understand the following as special cases: a. 100 can be thought of as a bundle of ten tens—called a " hundred."	Unit 2 Lessons 1, 2, 3, 4, 6, 7, 8, 9, 11; Unit 4 Lessons 3, 4, 7, 8, 9, 10, 12, 14; Unit 6 Lessons 1, 4
2.NBT.A.1.b	Understand that the three digits of a three-digit number represent amounts of hundreds, tens, and ones; e.g., 706 equals 7 hundreds, 0 tens, and 6 ones. Understand the following as special cases: • The numbers 100, 200, 300, 400, 500, 600, 700, 800, 900 refer to one, two, three, four, five, six, seven, eight, or nine hundreds (and 0 tens and 0 ones).	Unit 4 Lesson 7; Unit 6 Lessons 1, 4
2.NBT.A.2	Count within 1000; skip-count by 5s, 10s, and 100s.	Unit 1 Lesson 6; Unit 2 Lessons 1, 2, 3, 12, 15; Unit 4 Lesson 15; Unit 5 Lesson 2; Unit 6 Lessons 1, 4
2.NBT.A.3	Read and write numbers to 1000 using base-ten numerals, number names, and expanded form.	Unit 2 Lessons 1, 2, 3, 4, 5; Unit 6 Lessons 1, 2, 4
2.NBT.A.4	Compare two three-digit numbers based on meanings of the hundreds, tens, and ones digits, using >, =, and < symbols to record the results of comparisons.	Unit 2 Lessons 5, 15; Unit 3 Lesson 6; Unit 5 Lesson 10; Unit 6 Lessons 3, 15

■ **Major**　　■ **Supporting**　　■ **Additional**

2.NBT Number and Operations in Base Ten

Use place value understanding and properties of operations to add and subtract.

2.NBT.B.5	Fluently add and subtract within 100 using strategies based on place value, properties of operations, and/or the relationship between addition and subtraction.	Unit 1 Lessons 9, 16; Unit 2 Lessons 2, 4,13, 14, 15; Unit 3 Lesson 9; Unit 4 Lessons 3, 4, 5, 6, 11, 12, 13, 14, 15, 17, 18, 19, 20,21, 22, 23; Unit 5 Lessons 5, 7; Unit 6 Lessons 3, 8, 10, 15; Unit 7 Lessons 4, 5
2.NBT.B.6	Add up to four two-digit numbers using strategies based on place value and properties of operations.	Unit 1 Lesson 9; Unit 2 Lessons 6, 8, 9, 10, 14; Unit 4 Lessons 14, 15; Unit 7 Lessons 4, 5
2.NBT.B.7	Add and subtract within 1000, using concrete models or drawings and strategies based on place value, properties of operations, and/or the relationship between addition and subtraction; relate the strategy to a written method. Understand that in adding or subtracting three-digit numbers, one adds or subtracts hundreds and hundreds, tens and tens, ones and ones; and sometimes it is necessary to compose or decompose tens or hundreds.	Unit 2 Lessons 4, 6, 7, 8, 9, 10, 11, 14, 15; Unit 4 Lessons 1, 2, 3, 5, 6, 7, 8, 9, 10, 12, 13, 15, 16, 17, 23; Unit 6 Lessons 2, 5, 6, 7, 8, 9, 10, 11, 12, 13, 14, 15
2.NBT.B.8	Mentally add 10 or 100 to a given number 100–900, and mentally subtract 10 or 100 from a given number 100–900.	Unit 2 Lesson 4; Unit 6 Lessons 2, 4
2.NBT.B.9	Explain why addition and subtraction strategies work, using place value and the properties of operations.	Unit 1 Lessons 1, 3, 9; Unit 2 Lessons 2, 4, 6, 7, 8, 9, 10; Unit 4 Lessons 3, 4, 5, 6, 7, 8, 9, 10, 12, 14, 15, 16, 17, 18; Unit 6 Lessons 2, 5, 6, 7, 8, 9, 10, 11, 12, 13, 15

Common Core State Standards for Mathematical Content

2.MD Measurement and Data

Measure and estimate lengths in standard units.

2.MD.A.1	Measure the length of an object by selecting and using appropriate tools such as rulers, yardsticks, meter sticks, and measuring tapes.	Unit 3 Lessons 1, 2, 3, 4, 6, 7, 8, 9; Unit 4 Lesson 23; Unit 7 Lesson 1
2.MD.A.2	Measure the length of an object twice, using length units of different lengths for the two measurements; describe how the two measurements relate to the size of the unit chosen.	Unit 3 Lessons 7, 8, 9
2.MD.A.3	Estimate lengths using units of inches, feet, centimeters, and meters.	Unit 3 Lessons 3, 4, 6, 7, 8; Unit 4 Lesson 23
2.MD.A.4	Measure to determine how much longer one object is than another, expressing the length difference in terms of a standard length unit.	Unit 3 Lessons 1, 2, 6; Unit 4 Lesson 23

Relate addition and subtraction to length.

2.MD.B.5	Use addition and subtraction within 100 to solve word problems involving lengths that are given in the same units, e.g., by using drawings (such as drawings of rulers) and equations with a symbol for the unknown number to represent the problem.	Unit 4 Lesson 23; Unit 7 Lessons 3, 4, 5
2.MD.B.6	Represent whole numbers as lengths from 0 on a number line diagram with equally spaced points corresponding to the numbers 0, 1, 2, . . . , and represent whole-number sums and differences within 100 on a number line diagram.	Unit 7 Lessons 3, 5

Work with time and money.

2.MD.C.7	Tell and write time from analog and digital clocks to the nearest five minutes, using a.m. and p.m.	Unit 5 Lessons 1, 2
2.MD.C.8	Solve word problems involving dollar bills, quarters, dimes, nickels, and pennies, using $ and ¢ symbols appropriately. *Example: If you have 2 dimes and 3 pennies, how many cents do you have?*	Unit 2 Lessons 11, 12, 15; Unit 4 Lessons 1,2, 10, 15; Unit 6 Lesson 1

■ **Major**   ■ **Supporting**   ▪ **Additional**

© Houghton Mifflin Harcourt Publishing Company

2.MD Measurement and Data

Represent and interpret data.

2.MD.D.9	Generate measurement data by measuring lengths of several objects to the nearest whole unit, or by making repeated measurements of the same object. Show the measurements by making a line plot, where the horizontal scale is marked off in whole-number units.	Unit 3 Lessons 6, 7, 8
2.MD.D.10	Draw a picture graph and a bar graph (with single-unit scale) to represent a data set with up to four categories. Solve simple put-together, take-apart, and compare problems using information presented in a bar graph.	Unit 5 Lessons 3, 4, 5, 6, 7, 8, 9, 10

2.G Geometry

Reason with shapes and their attributes.

2.G.A.1	Recognize and draw shapes having specified attributes, such as a given number of angles or a given number of equal faces. Identify triangles, quadrilaterals, pentagons, hexagons, and cubes.	Unit 3 Lessons 2, 3, 4, 5, 9; Unit 7 Lessons 1, 2, 4
2.G.A.2	Partition a rectangle into rows and columns of same-size squares and count to find the total number of them.	Unit 7 Lessons 1, 6
2.G.A.3	Partition circles and rectangles into two, three, or four equal shares, describe the shares using the words *halves*, *thirds*, *half of*, *a third of*, etc., and describe the whole as two halves, three thirds, four fourths. Recognize that equal shares of identical wholes need not have the same shape.	Unit 5 Lesson 2; Unit 7 Lessons 1, 2, 6

Common Core State Standards for Mathematical Practice

MP1 Make sense of problems and persevere in solving them.

Mathematically proficient students start by explaining to themselves the meaning of a problem and looking for entry points to its solution. They analyze givens, constraints, relationships, and goals. They make conjectures about the form and meaning of the solution and plan a solution pathway rather than simply jumping into a solution attempt. They consider analogous problems, and try special cases and simpler forms of the original problem in order to gain insight into its solution. They monitor and evaluate their progress and change course if necessary. Older students might, depending on the context of the problem, transform algebraic expressions or change the viewing window on their graphing calculator to get the information they need. Mathematically proficient students can explain correspondences between equations, verbal descriptions, tables, and graphs or draw diagrams of important features and relationships, graph data, and search for regularity or trends. Younger students might rely on using concrete objects or pictures to help conceptualize and solve a problem. Mathematically proficient students check their answers to problems using a different method, and they continually ask themselves, "Does this make sense?" They can understand the approaches of others to solving complex problems and identify correspondences between different approaches.

Unit 1 Lessons 2, 4, 6, 7, 9, 10, 11, 12, 13, 14, 15, 16, 17, 18, 19, 20, 21
Unit 2 Lessons 1, 2, 3, 4, 5, 6, 7, 8, 9, 11, 12, 13, 14, 15
Unit 3 Lessons 1, 3, 6, 9
Unit 4 Lessons 1, 2, 3, 4, 5, 6, 7, 8, 9, 10, 11, 12, 13, 14, 16, 17, 18, 19, 20, 21, 22, 23
Unit 5 Lessons 1, 3, 4, 5, 6, 7, 8, 9, 10
Unit 6 Lessons 1, 4, 5, 8, 9, 10, 11, 12, 14, 15
Unit 7 Lessons 1, 2, 3, 4, 5, 6

MP2 Reason abstractly and quantitatively.

Mathematically proficient students make sense of quantities and their relationships in problem situations. They bring two complementary abilities to bear on problems involving quantitative relationships: the ability to *decontextualize*—to abstract a given situation and represent it symbolically and manipulate the representing symbols as if they have a life of their own, without necessarily attending to their referents—and the ability to *contextualize*, to pause as needed during the manipulation process in order to probe into the referents for the symbols involved. Quantitative reasoning entails habits of creating a coherent representation of the problem at hand, considering the units involved, attending to the meaning of quantities, not just how to compute them, and knowing and flexibly using different properties of operations and objects.

Unit 1 Lessons 1, 5, 7, 8, 9, 10, 11, 14, 21
Unit 2 Lessons 1, 3, 4, 5, 6, 7, 8, 9, 11, 12, 13, 14, 15
Unit 3 Lessons 1, 2, 3, 7, 8, 9
Unit 4 Lessons 1, 2, 3, 4, 5, 6, 7, 8, 9, 10, 11, 12, 13, 14, 15, 17, 19, 20, 22, 23
Unit 5 Lessons 1, 2, 5, 10
Unit 6 Lessons 1, 2, 4, 10, 12, 15
Unit 7 Lessons 1, 2, 3, 4, 5, 6

■ **Major**　■ **Supporting**　■ **Additional**

MP3 Construct viable arguments and critique the reasoning of others.

Mathematically proficient students understand and use stated assumptions, definitions, and previously established results in constructing arguments. They make conjectures and build a logical progression of statements to explore the truth of their conjectures. They are able to analyze situations by breaking them into cases, and can recognize and use counterexamples. They justify their conclusions, communicate them to others, and respond to the arguments of others. They reason inductively about data, making plausible arguments that take into account the context from which the data arose. Mathematically proficient students are also able to compare the effectiveness of two plausible arguments, distinguish correct logic or reasoning from that which is flawed, and—if there is a flaw in an argument—explain what it is. Elementary students can construct arguments using concrete referents such as objects, drawings, diagrams, and actions. Such arguments can make sense and be correct, even though they are not generalized or made formal until later grades. Later, students learn to determine domains to which an argument applies. Students at all grades can listen to or read the arguments of others, decide whether they make sense, and ask useful questions to clarify or improve the arguments.

Unit 1 Lessons 1, 3, 4, 6, 7, 8, 9, 10, 11, 12, 13, 14, 15, 16, 17, 18, 19, 20, 21
Unit 2 Lessons 2, 3, 4, 5, 6, 7, 8, 9, 10, 12, 13, 14, 15
Unit 3 Lessons 1, 2, 3, 4, 5, 6, 7, 8, 9
Unit 4 Lessons 1, 2, 3, 4, 5, 6, 7, 8, 9, 10, 11, 12, 13, 14, 15, 16, 17, 18, 19, 20, 21, 22, 23
Unit 5 Lessons 1, 2, 3, 4, 5, 6, 7, 8, 9, 10
Unit 6 Lessons 1, 2, 3, 4, 5, 6, 7, 8, 9, 10, 11, 12, 13, 14, 15
Unit 7 Lessons 1, 2, 3, 4, 5, 6

MP4 Model with mathematics.

Mathematically proficient students can apply the mathematics they know to solve problems arising in everyday life, society, and the workplace. In early grades, this might be as simple as writing an addition equation to describe a situation. In middle grades, a student might apply proportional reasoning to plan a school event or analyze a problem in the community. By high school, a student might use geometry to solve a design problem or use a function to describe how one quantity of interest depends on another. Mathematically proficient students who can apply what they know are comfortable making assumptions and approximations to simplify a complicated situation, realizing that these may need revision later. They are able to identify important quantities in a practical situation and map their relationships using such tools as diagrams, two-way tables, graphs, flowcharts and formulas. They can analyze those relationships mathematically to draw conclusions. They routinely interpret their mathematical results in the context of the situation and reflect on whether the results make sense, possibly improving the model if it has not served its purpose.

Unit 1 Lessons 10, 11, 12, 13, 15, 16, 17, 18, 19, 20, 21
Unit 2 Lessons 4, 6, 7, 11, 12, 14, 15
Unit 3 Lessons 6, 7, 8, 9
Unit 4 Lessons 3, 4, 5, 7, 10, 12, 13, 18, 19, 20, 21, 23
Unit 5 Lessons 3, 5, 8, 9, 10
Unit 6 Lessons 9, 11, 14, 15
Unit 7 Lessons 3, 6

Common Core State Standards for Mathematical Practice

MP5 Use appropriate tools strategically.

Mathematically proficient students consider the available tools when solving a mathematical problem. These tools might include pencil and paper, concrete models, a ruler, a protractor, a calculator, a spreadsheet, a computer algebra system, a statistical package, or dynamic geometry software. Proficient students are sufficiently familiar with tools appropriate for their grade or course to make sound decisions about when each of these tools might be helpful, recognizing both the insight to be gained and their limitations. For example, mathematically proficient high school students analyze graphs of functions and solutions generated using a graphing calculator. They detect possible errors by strategically using estimation and other mathematical knowledge. When making mathematical models, they know that technology can enable them to visualize the results of varying assumptions, explore consequences, and compare predictions with data. Mathematically proficient students at various grade levels are able to identify relevant external mathematical resources, such as digital content located on a website, and use them to pose or solve problems. They are able to use technological tools to explore and deepen their understanding of concepts.

Unit 1 Lessons 3, 4, 6, 20, 21
Unit 2 Lessons 1, 2, 3, 4, 5, 8, 12, 13, 14, 15
Unit 3 Lessons 1, 2, 3, 5, 6, 7, 8, 9
Unit 4 Lessons 1, 2, 3, 4, 7, 8, 9, 11, 15, 18, 23
Unit 5 Lessons 1, 2, 5, 10
Unit 6 Lessons 1, 2, 5, 7, 10, 15
Unit 7 Lessons 1, 2, 3, 6

MP6 Attend to precision.

Mathematically proficient students try to communicate precisely to others. They try to use clear definitions in discussion with others and in their own reasoning. They state the meaning of the symbols they choose, including using the equal sign consistently and appropriately. They are careful about specifying units of measure and labeling axes to clarify the correspondence with quantities in a problem. They calculate accurately and efficiently, expressing numerical answers with a degree of precision appropriate for the problem context. In the elementary grades, students give carefully formulated explanations to each other. By the time they reach high school they have learned to examine claims and make explicit use of definitions.

Unit 1 Lessons 1, 2, 3, 4, 5, 6, 7, 8, 9, 10, 11, 12, 13, 14, 15, 16, 17, 18, 19, 20, 21
Unit 2 Lessons 1, 2, 3, 4, 5, 6, 7, 8, 9, 10, 11, 12, 13, 14, 15
Unit 3 Lessons 1, 2, 3, 4, 5, 6, 7, 8, 9
Unit 4 Lessons 1, 2, 3, 4, 5, 6, 7, 8, 9, 10, 11, 12, 13, 14, 15, 16, 17, 18, 19, 20, 21, 22, 23
Unit 5 Lessons 1, 2, 3, 4, 5, 6, 7, 8, 9, 10
Unit 6 Lessons 1, 2, 3, 4, 5, 6, 7, 8, 9, 10, 11, 12, 13, 14, 15
Unit 7 Lessons 1, 2, 3, 4, 5, 6

■ Major   ■ Supporting   ■ Additional

© Houghton Mifflin Harcourt Publishing Company

MP7 Look for and make use of structure.

Mathematically proficient students look closely to discern a pattern or structure. Young students, for example, might notice that three and seven more is the same amount as seven and three more, or they may sort a collection of shapes according to how many sides the shapes have. Later, students will see 7×8 equals the well remembered $7 \times 5 + 7 \times 3$, in preparation for learning about the distributive property. In the expression $x^2 + 9x + 14$, older students can see the 14 as 2×7 and the 9 as $2 + 7$. They recognize the significance of an existing line in a geometric figure and can use the strategy of drawing an auxiliary line for solving problems. They also can step back for an overview and shift perspective. They can see complicated things, such as some algebraic expressions, as single objects or as being composed of several objects. For example, they can see $5 - 3(x - y)^2$ as 5 minus a positive number times a square and use that to realize that its value cannot be more than 5 for any real numbers x and y.

Unit 1 Lessons 1, 2, 5, 6, 9, 13, 17, 18, 19, 21
Unit 2 Lessons 1, 2, 3, 4, 6, 10, 11, 12, 15
Unit 3 Lessons 1, 3, 4, 5, 6, 7, 8, 9
Unit 4 Lessons 1, 2, 7, 13, 17, 19, 21, 23
Unit 5 Lessons 2, 6, 7, 10
Unit 6 Lessons 4, 12, 13, 15
Unit 7 Lessons 2, 6

MP8 Look for and express regularity in repeated reasoning.

Mathematically proficient students notice if calculations are repeated, and look both for general methods and for shortcuts. Upper elementary students might notice when dividing 25 by 11 that they are repeating the same calculations over and over again, and conclude they have a repeating decimal. By paying attention to the calculation of slope as they repeatedly check whether points are on the line through (1, 2) with slope 3, middle school students might abstract the equation $(y - 2)/(x - 1) = 3$. Noticing the regularity in the way terms cancel when expanding $(x - 1)(x + 1)$, $(x - 1)(x^2 + x + 1)$, and $(x - 1)(x^3 + x^2 + x + 1)$ might lead them to the general formula for the sum of a geometric series. As they work to solve a problem, mathematically proficient students maintain oversight of the process, while attending to the details. They continually evaluate the reasonableness of their intermediate results.

Unit 1 Lessons 2, 6, 7, 21
Unit 2 Lessons 5, 10, 11, 15
Unit 3 Lessons 1, 2, 7, 8, 9
Unit 4 Lessons 4, 8, 13, 23
Unit 5 Lessons 2, 10
Unit 6 Lessons 2, 4, 7, 8, 12, 15
Unit 7 Lessons 1, 2, 6

Index

Index

halves, 371–372, 375–376
thirds, 371–372, 375–376

Equal sign (=), 29, 97–98, 317

Equations. *See also* **Addition;
Algebra; Problem Types; Subtraction.**
chains, 29
relate to Math Mountains, 3, 66–67,
227–228, 229, 230. *See also*
Subtraction.
situation and solution, S1–S3
unknown addend or partner, 30,
230, 237–240, 333–334. *See also*
Subtraction.
unknown total, 13–14, 30, 47–48,
67, 96, 227–228, 241–242,
243–245, 390
vertical form, 30

Estimation
length, 149–152, 163–164, 170, 173

Even numbers, 25–26

Expanded form, 93, 316

Expanded Method
in subtraction. *See* Algorithms.

F

**Family Letter, 1–2, 7–8, 37–38, 85–86,
101–102, 139–140, 159–160, 189–
190, 261–262, 275–276, 307–308,
325–326, 337–338, 365–366**

Fluency activities and games
New Ten Challenge, 125–126
Ungroup Challenge, 223–224

Fluency Check. *See* **Addition;
Assessment; Subtraction.**

Fluency practice
addition within 20, 34, 48, 104

addition within 100, 123–124,
231, 238, 246, 284, 318, 334,
342
subtraction within 20, 34, 48, 104
subtraction within 100, 221–222,
231, 238, 246, 334, 342

**Focus on Math Practices, 297–298,
391–392**

Fourths, 371–372, 375–376

Fractions
Equal shares, 371–372, 375–376,
391–392
Time (half-hour), 270

G

Geometry. *See also* **Measurement.**
angles, 145–148
right, 145–146, 149–150
attributes
corners (angles), 145
faces, 155, 156
sides, 145–148
plane shapes
circle, 376
classify, 145–148, 156
compare, 146–148
compose, 179–180
decompose, 179–180, 369–372,
375–376, 391–392
distance around (perimeter),
149–152
hexagon, 148, 156, 179–180
measurement of, 149–152
pentagon, 148, 156, 179–180
quadrilaterals, 148, 156, 179–180
rectangle, 146, 150, 155, 156,
369–372, 375–376
square, 145–146, 149, 155, 156,
376

N

© Houghton Mifflin Harcourt Publishing Company

Index

Q

R

S

Index

© Houghton Mifflin Harcourt Publishing Company

Index

Illustrator: Josh Brill

Did you ever try to use shapes to draw animals like the platypus on the cover?

Over the last 10 years Josh has been using geometric shapes to design his animals. His aim is to keep the animal drawings simple and use color to make them appealing.

Add some color to the platypus Josh drew. Then try drawing a cat or dog or some other animal using the shapes below.

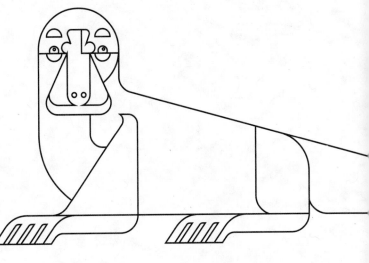

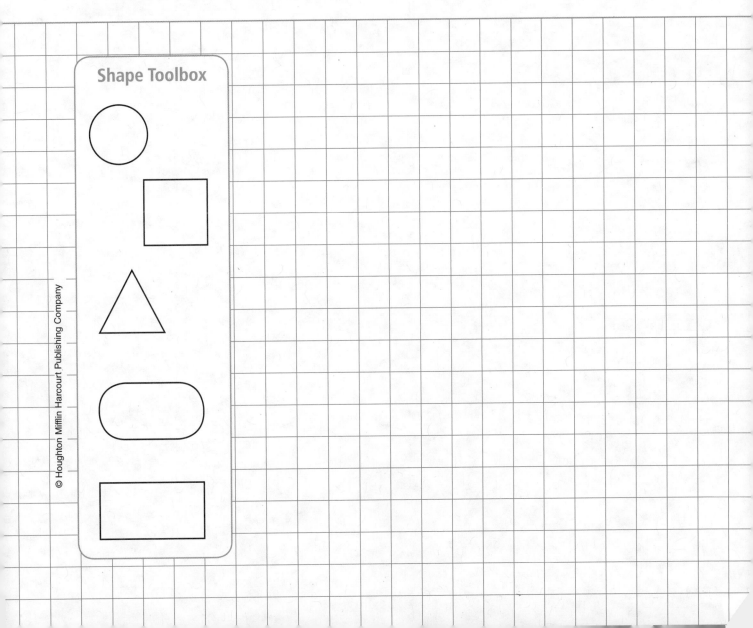

Shape Toolbox